D1371944

Whether you are a newlywed or have been married fifty years, Dan and Linda Wilson's book *Lovemaking* will awaken your love life to greater heights of desire, passion, and playfulness. They masterfully illuminate the beauty of sexual intimacy within the context of a covenantal marriage relationship. God created sex, and he wants us to enjoy it! If you want to experience new levels of intimacy with your spouse, this book is for you.

—**KRIS VALLOTTON**
Senior Associate Leader, Bethel Church, Redding, CA
Cofounder of Bethel School of Supernatural Ministry
Author of ten books, including *The Supernatural Ways of Royalty* and *Spirit Wars*

Dan and Linda Wilson are a couple who truly live what they preach, and as a result, they carry Kingdom authority that flows through love. In this book, they cover a sensitive and personal topic that many would not want to give attention to, and yet it is so needed. I sincerely commend Dan and Linda Wilson to you.

—**PATRICIA KING**
Founder, XP Ministries

Lovemaking uses a thoroughly biblical foundation to illuminate the physical, emotional, spiritual, and *playful* aspects of God's design for sex in marriage. From Scripture to anatomy to practical tips, authors Dan and Linda Wilson provide helpful information and encouragement to take your marriage bed from ho-hum to heavenly. Definitely a recommended read!

—J. PARKER

Blogger at www.hotholyhumorous.com and author of
Sex Savvy: A Lovemaking Guide for Christian Wives and
Intimacy Revealed: 52 Devotions to Enhance Sex in Marriage

Reading *Lovemaking* has left me blessed and thankful to God. I fully recommend this book to my own children and their friends who are of marrying age, as well as all couples who are already married. Read this book and keep it on your side table in your bedroom.

I am Mexican and come from a culture in which we were taught that talking about sex, thinking about sex, and especially having sex was a sin. Once one gets married, the idea that it is all sinful is so engrained in your mind, you can't distinguish between merely having sex and making love.

Today, it is important that people come to understand the revelation this book, so full of God's Word, gives: That making love, in all of its meaning, is holy, is fun, and is part of the gift that God gives to married couples.

I am so excited to learn in these later decades of our lives (I'm in my early 50s), that our maturity helps us become better lovers! It is so exciting to think that my husband and I can have a new way to make holy and satisfying love. I am convinced that God has given us this privilege.

—INGRID FIEHN-SERVIN

Healing Rooms Ministries, regional director for Northeast Mexico

Dr. Dan and Linda Wilson have written another outstanding book for couples...but this one is very different! *Lovemaking* deals with a subject that is too often considered taboo within the church. We're so glad the Wilson's were willing to pull back the sheets in order to share their straight-forward, honest, and practical advice that will help many couples succeed in the bedroom and beyond! Sex was, is, and always will be God's idea for lasting marriages. We only wish this book had been available years ago when we first got married. It is an excellent reference for newlyweds and any married couple that would like to ignite their passion and feel like newlyweds all over again!

—JOSHUA & JANET MILLS
Lovers, authors, and international conference speakers
www.joshuamills.com

God created everything—including sex. *Lovemaking* is one of the most biblically sound and healthiest books on the market about sex and marriage. Dr. Dan and Linda Wilson do an outstanding job at conveying God's original design and intent for the most extravagant, creative, spicy, intimate sexual expressions between husband and wife. I highly recommend this book to every couple wanting to strengthen their sexual intimacy and marriage!

—CHÉ AHN
Harvest Apostolic Center
Founding pastor, HRock Church, Pasadena, CA
President, Harvest International Ministry

I appreciate Dan and Linda explaining sex as part of a healthy marriage; great sex requires a great marriage. *Lovemaking* is the perfect book for any couple looking to experience sex as the wonderful adventure God intended.

—**PAUL H. BYERLY**
Marriage and sex educator
www.the-generous-husband.com, www.themarriagebed.com

Dan and Linda Wilson have been personal friends of mine for several years. Their hearts are as pure as purified gold. They have such a hunger for the body of Christ to have healthy and fulfilling marriages in every area of marriage. Their book is another way to help marriages today be healed and whole.

—**JOAN HUNTER**
Author and healing evangelist

I recommend Dan and Linda Wilson and their ministry. They are people of integrity and anointing.

—**RANDY CLARK, D. MIN.**
Founder and president of Global Awakening and the
Apostolic Network of Global Awakening

Thank you Dan and Linda for your courage to write this informative, practical and just downright fun book! I believe it will be used to restore and deepen the adventure of sexual intimacy in many marriages.

—**STEVE FISH**
Senior Leader, Convergence Church, Fort Worth, Texas

Lovemaking

10 Secrets to Extravagant Intimacy in Marriage

DR. DAN & LINDA WILSON

BroadStreet
PUBLISHING

BroadStreet Publishing Group, LLC
Racine, Wisconsin, USA
www.broadstreetpublishing.com

Lovemaking
10 Secrets to Extravagant Intimacy in Marriage

© 2015 Dr. Dan and Linda Wilson

ISBN-13: 978-1-4245-5005-0 (hardcover)
ISBN-13: 978-1-4245-5021-0 (e-book)

All rights reserved. No part of this book may be reproduced in any form, except for brief quotations in printed reviews, without permission in writing from the publisher.

All Scripture quotations, unless otherwise indicated, are from the *Holy Bible, New International Version*. *NIV*. Copyright © 1973, 1978, 1984 by International Bible Society. Used by permission of Zondervan. All rights reserved. Scripture quotations marked NKJV are from the New King James Version. Copyright © 1982 by Thomas Nelson, Inc. Used by permission. All rights reserved. Scripture quotations marked MSG are from *The Message*. Copyright © 1993, 1994, 1995, 1996, 2000, 2001, 2002. Used by permission of NavPress Publishing Group. Scripture quotations marked KJV are from the King James Version of the Holy Bible, which is in the Public Domain. Scripture quotations marked TPT are from *Matthew: Our Loving King, The Passion Translation*, Copyright © 2015 BroadStreet Publishing Group, LLC, www.thepassiontranslation. com. Used by permission. All rights reserved. *Note that emphasis within Scripture is from the author and not in the original text.*

Cover by Garborg Design Works, Inc. | www.garborgdesign.com
Interior by Katherine Lloyd | www.theDESKonline.com

Stock or custom editions of BroadStreet Publishing titles may be purchased in bulk for educational, business, ministry, fundraising, or sales promotional use. For information, please e-mail info@ broadstreetpublishing.com.

Printed in China

15 16 17 18 19 20   5 4 3 2 1

Contents

Imagination plays a huge part in lovemaking. Sexual fantasy should be pure and honoring to your spouse and to God. Using your sanctified imagination will add spice to your sex life.

Regardless of differences in your sexual appetites and physical changes in your bodies, both you and your mate can be sexy and satisfied as you meet each other's needs. Recognize and celebrate your differences. You are a team. Together you can win!

Our bodies change. Sometimes we must literally reposition— adapting the way we play to accommodate health changes and aging. Sexual play can still be fantastic in the midst of physical challenges.

Embracing divine order (God and then spouse) makes room for you to love and be loved. He designed you as a sexual being. You were made for this!

Lovemaking is not about sex. It is really all about love. Each person is created in the image of the Great Lover.

Introduction

G od loves sex. He created it, He encourages it, and He enhances it. Allowing, even inviting, the Holy Spirit into
this most intimate place in your marriage will bring great fun
and excitement into your relationship. With Christ in us, we
are designed to be the greatest lovers on earth!

Perhaps you are currently disillusioned with your sex
life—you may have possibly given up hope that your marriage
could be rich and satisfying. If that is you, then this book is
for you! Or maybe you are one of the couples who enjoy a
thriving sex life in your marriage. If that is the case, then we
celebrate with you! Regardless of where you would rate your
sexual intimacy in the continuum—from poor to good to
totally awesome—we pray these *ten secrets* will stimulate you
(pun intended) to go for more. Let's go beyond great, all the
way to astounding.

Great skill is needed to build a great marriage, and we
believe that God wants you to be a skilled spouse in the sexual
arena. The enemy uses sexual dissatisfaction to bring harm to
marriages, and so it is God's supernatural power that releases
us to become the expert lovers God created us to be. Through
the supernatural touch of God, we discover the value of

holiness, we are set free to fully enjoy sex in marriage, and we are transformed to become husbands and wives who love without restraint.

Utilizing my (Dan's) medical expertise, our thirty-three years of marriage, and true stories from friends and people we've counseled (whose names are changed to protect their privacy), this book will encourage you to know your tools and how to use them to design and build a beautiful, satisfying relationship.

At the close of each chapter you will find "prescriptions" for adding a little spice to your play. We hope you will have a lot of fun following the doctor's orders.

As you begin reading, ask the Holy Spirit to renew your mind. Ask Him to free you from anything preventing you from being a great giver or receiver of love. And ask God to teach you how to be the extravagant lover you were created to be. You were made in His image, and He is all about love.

Holy really is fun!

Dan & Linda

1

Play

Kelli and Jim had a huge heart for missions. They loved God. They loved people. They loved learning about different cultures. And they loved their large family. For years they had desired to go on a short-term mission trip, but babies and the demands of family had made it difficult to get away.

An amazing invitation came for Kelli and Jim to go to Mongolia during the winter. They were asked to teach, preach, and do prayer ministry with church leaders there. Immediately their hearts leaped with a resounding yes!

Preparations began right away—obtaining warm clothing, arranging for childcare, and scheduling Jim to be away from work. All the details quickly fell into place. Before they knew it, Kelli and Jim were on a plane to the bitterly cold land of Mongolia. These two really loved each other. Getting away childless for a weekend had proven difficult throughout the years, and now they were getting away for two weeks without children! Woo-hoo!

The bitter cold almost took their breath away when they landed in Mongolia. The ministry was intense, often teaching and praying until the wee hours of the morning. But Kelli and

Jim were free from a baby's cry or a toddler climbing into bed with them. Even with the jet lag and fatigue, these two snuggled up in their warm bed making great use of each other's body heat.

Upon their return home, Kelli called to tell us about their trip. The first words out of her mouth were, "It was so great to be alone that we had sex every night—ten nights in a row!" Even with all the amazing God stories from the trip, the uninterrupted time for play was a highlight for these two lovers. Kelli and Jim went far away from home to serve as missionaries in a foreign land and had far more fun than they anticipated. They were delighted to discover that playing together was as important a part of the journey as was the "spiritual" work that was planned.

In this book we will use "play" interchangeably with having sex. But play within the context of marriage is much more than sexual encounter. It is a lifestyle marked by exuberance in the intentional pursuit of joy. All forms of play are of great value because play reactivates the child within each one of us.

> *God knows that childlikeness is important*
> *throughout our lives, and He celebrates with us*
> *as it is released to husbands and wives who play.*[1]

---

1 Throughout this book we talk about the *playground* of marriage and the importance of being *childlike*. But in no way do we endorse underage sex, which is both immoral and illegal. If you struggle with these terms due to past hurt or abuse, please invite God to heal you and redeem these concepts to His original and pure intent.

Childlike Play

A familiar church Sunday school song is "Jesus Loves the Little Children." This simple song brings joy to those of any age who remain young at heart. In our hurried rush toward adulthood, many of us lose our appreciation for the merits of being a child. But God makes it clear in Scripture that there is much during this early season of life that is of great worth, and that should be pursued in our latter years.

In rebuking His disciples, Jesus made an astonishing statement: "Anyone who will not receive the kingdom of God like a little child will never enter it" (Mark 10:15). And Jesus told Nicodemus, "I tell you the truth, no one can see the kingdom of God unless he is born again" (John 3:3). There are several characteristics of being childlike that God values greatly. One of them, in particular, is naïveté.

Adults are insultingly called naïve when they are inexperienced in the ways of the world. It is necessary for us to understand *some* aspects of the world's ways, but there is no need for us to participate in the world's dark view of sexuality. Satan has twisted and distorted the beauty of sex in an effort to steal, kill, and destroy a wonderful gift from our loving Father. But Jesus came that we may experience the fullness of life the way He designed in the beginning. For those who are married, sexual play has a vital role in the abundant life God wants us to enjoy.

Romans 16:19 tells us to be wise about what is good, and innocent (naïve, inexperienced in, deliberately avoiding) what is evil.

*A degree of naïveté is part of a healthy ambiance
for satisfying sex-play. At any age it is a good thing
for us to be innocent about the evil offered by
the kingdom of darkness.*

Participating with evil blocks our ability to receive the impartation of perfect love from the Father and decreases our capacity to share this love with our mate.

On the other hand, when partners focus on excellent play in the marriage bed, they are being "wise about what is good." Nothing is more erotic than husband and wife, filled with the love of heaven, purely and freely enjoying one another in the way God intended. In fact, God is delighted when His children share in the good pleasures of sexual play.

Every father loves to watch his children having fun. Our Father in heaven is the best of all dads—full of goodness and mercy, and abounding in love. Seeing us play, both sexually and otherwise, brings a huge smile to God's face. His desire is that we would satisfy each other during our years of being united together in marriage. He truly wants His children to enjoy every gift they have received from His loving hands.

Being God's children, it is essential for us to learn how to play—and play well. More important than knowing the specific details of how to play sexually is the attitude with which we approach the subject. Husbands and wives who approach physical intimacy with wonder and enthusiasm will not be disappointed. The simplest of romantic games can be amazingly fun when played with one's lifetime lover and friend.

One of our favorite romantic games involves searching for and riding Ferris wheels. In ministry we travel to many nations of the world. Whether in India, Uganda, China, or New Zealand, our eyes are constantly on the lookout for these towering, turning wheels of light. Riding them brings us joyous laughter, beautiful pictures to be taken, and memories to recall. We hold hands as the wheel takes us high up into the air, squeal together while passing over the top, and giggle like children all the way down. Our life in marriage is made richer and more full through opportunities for experiencing the whole gambit of playing together as darling friends.

In covenant marriage, God has created the wonderful and astonishing opportunity for spouses to wholeheartedly experience the pleasures of overtly sexual play.

Within safe boundaries there is freedom for husband and wife to enjoy each other fully, in body, soul, and spirit. Nothing can compare with the joy available within the safe playground of marriage.

God's Playground

In our book *7 Secrets of a Supernatural Marriage*, we share a story about a school playground that was adjacent to a busy city street and the need for safety in order for the children to feel the freedom to play.

There was no fence separating the two; both children and teachers could sense the danger that was present. In this atmosphere, kindergarten students remained very close to their teacher during recess instead of playing in the big open field. Although this assured their safety, it deprived them of the many areas and activities available on the playground. The children were unable to fully enjoy recess because the playground felt treacherous to them.

The school leaders, aware of the risk of having children play so close to the street, had a sturdy fence constructed around the borders of the playground. Soon the children were running, bouncing balls, swinging, and exuberantly playing on every square inch of the property. They were full of joy and laughter because they had a safe place to play. What had seemed scary to them was now fun because of the barrier that separated them from the dangerous traffic on the street.

Marriage is very much like that properly fenced playground. In the written word of the Bible, by direct revelation, and through the personal leading of the Holy Spirit, God establishes wise, strong, protective barriers around His children's marital playground. All activity within these secured boundaries is righteous and good, conforming to God's perfect will. Anything outside of these boundaries is unholy, unrighteous, and outside of His will. Everything outside is the street we're not allowed to play in because of the danger involved.[2]

---

2 Dan and Linda Wilson, *7 Secrets of a Supernatural Marriage: The Joy of Spirit-Led Intimacy* (Racine, WI: BroadStreet Publishing, 2014), 109–110.

God's playground is safe because it is holy. We elaborate
on this point further in *7 Secrets of a Supernatural Marriage*:

> As we grow in holiness, we honor God as our Cre-
> ator and honor the beauty and perfection of His plan.
> Our holiness greatly pleases the Father. This is why, in
> establishing the Law with the children of Israel, God
> repeatedly told Moses, "Speak to the entire assembly of
> Israel and say to them: 'Be holy because I, the Lord your
> God, am holy'" (Leviticus 19:2; 11:44–45).
>
> A marriage truly connected to the holiness of God is
> an amazing thing. In this kind of relationship we can let
> down all our defenses and just *be* instead of always *doing*
> and trying to perform. We fulfill the destiny God created
> us to enjoy as we walk in the holiness of marriage. In this
> place all is freely shared and no barrier exists between
> husband and wife. There is no fear about what the other
> person might think, nor is there any doubt concerning
> the motivations of each other's actions. In God's play-
> ground called marriage, we are encouraged to love deeply
> and freely, to laugh and to play, without fear of the dan-
> gers that lie outside of these God-ordained boundaries.[3]

God created the covenant of marriage to be the safest and
most pleasurable of all playgrounds. Within this context we
are given permission from heaven to sexually "go for it" with

---

3 Ibid., 110–111.

our mate. We are designed with the ability to extravagantly give and receive love through intimate relations that demonstrate the extreme oneness of holy matrimony.

Loving God Makes Us Better Lovers

We enter the path toward experiencing full sexual satisfaction when we decide to "go for it" with God. Psalm 37:4 encourages us with these words: "Delight yourself in the LORD and he will give you the desires of your heart." God lovingly created both men and women with strong sexual drives. In the heart of husbands and wives there is an intense desire to enjoy the pleasures of sex, both for procreation and for recreation.

> *God wants us to fully enjoy*
> *sex together within marriage.*

But sex cannot be our primary goal in life. It is only when our first priority is to delight ourselves in Him that He will give us the other desires of our hearts. The Spirit of God will open the door to experiencing sexual relations in marriage that truly satisfy.

Pursuing God with all your heart, mind, soul, and strength is by far the best way husbands and wives can prepare themselves to go for great sex with their marriage partners. Let's state this in a very simple way: Loving God makes us better lovers. When we "seek first his kingdom and his righteousness," Jesus promises that "all these things" will be given to us as well (Matthew 6:33). Outside of the necessities of life Jesus is referring to here, we believe this also includes a better sex life with your spouse.

The fact is that God created sex—He likes it and wants it to be fully enjoyed by His children. We share God's enthusiasm for sex within marriage by urging couples to play freely, play often, and play with enthusiasm. But the important part is to just play!

Sometimes we have a tendency to take things really important to us—like relating intimately with God or romantically pleasing our lover—too seriously. God prefers that we search for Him with the wonder of a little child rather than approach Him as qualified experts who have nothing left to learn. The same can be said of romantic pursuit in marriage.

In writing this book we were considering using the title *Expert Lover*, until we read a passage from Bill Johnson's book *Hosting the Presence*. Relating the word *expert* to our relationship with God, Bill writes:

> Why do you think the new moves of God almost always start with people who don't know what they are doing? At least in part, we limit God to our present understanding of how God moves, all while praying that God would do a new thing among us. What we know can keep us from what we need to know if we don't remain a novice. *When we become experts we have chosen where we level off in our maturity.* He still requires that primary advancements in the Kingdom be made through childlikeness.[4]

---

4 Bill Johnson, *Hosting the Presence: Unveiling Heaven's Agenda* (Shippensburg, PA: Destiny Image, 2012), 116. Emphasis ours.

Once we consider ourselves to be expert lovers, our thirst for what is better may be quenched, stopping the childlike pursuit to explore beyond our present level of experience. What is good can become the greatest obstacle to reaching what is best. While we should remain thankful for the level of intimacy already enjoyed in marriage, life in the supernatural realm of God affords opportunity to progress into oneness and satisfaction beyond the limits of normal expectation. God's desire is to bless us as husbands and wives in ways that cannot be imagined. It brings Him great joy to "knock our socks off" as we discover higher levels of shared pleasure in lovemaking.

Perhaps it is best to use the term "expert lover" as a descriptive title for God Himself. We will never reach the higher levels of lovemaking through the study of techniques or the application of sexual information. Only through actively seeking intimacy with God can we obtain what is needed to fully embrace intimate play in marriage. In His presence we receive the character and gifts required to love our partners as imitators of the One who *is* love.

*God is **the** expert lover who is working in and through us*
to produce satisfying sexual encounters with our mate.

The Holy Spirit leads and empowers us to love beyond mere human capacity. We are released into new dimensions of intimacy that can be shared and enjoyed only in the context of a covenant marriage. Through sexual play we are given a brief taste on earth of the astonishing oneness we will experience in heaven.

As one flesh in marriage, we are constantly in pursuit of becoming the ultimate lovers God created us to be. May we never level off! Joyfully and playfully, we continue to reach for what is next. There are no limitations in the supernatural realm of God. With the Spirit of God as our teacher, there is always more to learn. Each step toward the goal can be full of excitement and joy.

The Honeymoon Is Never Over

There are many things we actively hope for in marriage. One is that God would keep our desire strong for one another, so that we will enjoy intimate play for a lifetime. It is commonly believed that after a period of months—certainly, by the end of the first year—"the honeymoon is over." To this we passionately say, "No! We do not agree!" Men and women never outgrow the need for play nor the excitement and wonder of the honeymoon phase. In fact, it is a wonderful ambition in marriage to play together throughout the years.

Watching our oldest son get married was an interesting time. Our emotions were all over the place—grieving that our family would never be the same again but experiencing the joy of adding a new member. Our son had grown up and was starting his own family now. Then the thought hit us: "Our son is going on his honeymoon. We can also go on a honeymoon! In fact, we are on a perpetual honeymoon!"

Then we began to think about it more. A hammock on a beach. Strolls along the sand at the water's edge. Seeing the brilliant stars at night away from the city lights. Long chats recalling family memories. Some laughter. Some tears. Watching seagulls fly by. Dreaming together. Time away from work. What a great time for rekindling romance! We love our sons (and their beautiful wives and our gorgeous grandkids), but how amazing it is to have time alone. The empty nest can be fabulous.

Hammocks were designed for only two people, and there's always a little sense of adventure with a hammock. Can we both get on it without flipping over? Whoever gets on first has to carefully scoot over, trying to make room for number two. Can anything be more romantic than stargazing on a cold night, snuggled up with a blanket on a hammock? And big decisions must be made: Should we lie with heads at the same end or at opposite ends? There are certainly advantages to both. Maybe we could do both on different nights.

We are now thirty-three years into our marriage and we are still honeymooning! Now, if we could only find a place to hang a hammock in our backyard.

The Need to Play

Deep within each of us God placed a desire—even a *need*—to play. He put it there because He thought it was important.

The value of play does not decrease with time. In fact, it adds zest to life at any age.

Men and women join together in marriage for a variety of reasons: love, companionship, financial stability, producing children, or even societal expectations. Our God-given desire to play is a common and powerful motivation for entering this lifelong commitment. This is seen in the lighthearted teasing that goes on when couples are getting to know one another during courtship. It is then acted out more passionately with consummation of full sexual encounter once the couple is married. When the important element of play is missing, however, it can be devastating to the relationship.

In counseling we have encountered many married couples with serious problems in the area of sexual play. It is not unusual to hear that one spouse is unwilling to commit to this kind of intense emotional and physical intimacy. What begins with fear during the honeymoon can actually turn into frigidity that lasts for decades. The consequences of unmet play needs through the years can be tragic for both partners. The one who is unwilling to play and the one who is disappointed by play's absence are equally injured.

There is often confusion among Christian wives, and sometimes husbands, as to God's view of intimate play in marriage. Many questions arise that need to be answered: Should I enjoy something that for years was called sin? Can I enjoy sexual excitement and still be holy before the Lord? Can I be "good," and also be good at sex?

We love this excerpt from an article written by Julie Sibert titled "3 Tips on Having a Great Orgasm."

Honestly, I think this is one of the biggest stumbling blocks, especially for Christian wives. For some reason, we often associate intense sexual pleasure with sin. No wonder so many wives resist it or are scared of it.

Strive to walk in the truth, though. When you are enjoying sexual pleasure in an exclusive God-honoring sexual relationship with your husband, you are pleasing God, not disappointing Him.

So when you feel that sexual sensation that really can't be put into words, focus on it and lean into it. Receive it for what it is and be grateful for it.

Not only is this good for you, but it's good for your husband too. If he is like most husbands, he wants to see his wife in the grips of intense sexual pleasure. It turns him on to turn you on.[5]

God wants you to play with enthusiasm and enjoy success! He created you with a passionate desire to pursue intimacy with your mate and the capacity to enjoy each encounter. You were wired to both give and receive pleasure through sexual play.

Marriage is intended to be the most intimate of all playgrounds.

---

5   Julie Sibert, "3 Tips on Having a Great Orgasm," Hot, Holy, and Humorous: http://hotholyhumorous.com/2013/06/3-tips-on-having-a-great-orgasm (accessed 3/3/2015).

Within the safe boundaries of marriage we
are invited to explore the wonders of sensuality,
yet remain pure before the Lord as we experience the
joys of touching, caressing, loving, and being loved.

Husband or wife, whether you're newly married or have been married for years, may your marriage be blessed by the advice of a wise king from long ago:

Bless your fresh-flowing fountain!
Enjoy the wife you married as a young man!
Lovely as an angel, beautiful as a rose—
don't ever quit taking delight in her body.
Never take her love for granted!
(Proverbs 5:18–19, MSG)

Play joyfully.
Play often.
Play with abandon.
And play well!

DR. DAN'S PRESCRIPTIONS FOR PLAY

* Share a chocolate truffle or your favorite sweet together! Savor it using all of your senses to get the most out of every calorie.
* Shower with your spouse. Use soap liberally to be sure every one of your partner's parts is clean.

* Set up a scavenger hunt for your mate. The prize at the end is new undies for him and for her.
* Schedule a playdate with your mate.

2

Liberate

Here is a letter we received from a joyful wife after finding sexual freedom in an area that many are too embarrassed to even discuss:

Oh, happy day—the day I was set free from sexual bondage. Having grown up in a sweet Christian home, I had developed a pretty strong religious spirit that told me what good Christian ladies did and did not do in the bedroom. Being ladylike was more important to me than being sexually satisfied. Following your recommendation, I investigated an online blog discussing holy sex. I didn't know that such blogs existed. God used this particular day's post to set me free.

I had suffered from disgust with the idea of oral sex. Tom was so great to me all those years, never asking me to do anything I was uncomfortable with sexually although I was well aware that this was something he wanted to explore. Actually, I was quite happy to please him in this way. The aversion was in allowing him to please me—until I read this particular blog.

I learned that day about how the husband feels strong and sexy when he satisfies his wife, how most often the wife cannot reach orgasm without oral or manual stimulation, how God designed the clitoris for pleasure, and how pleasing it is for my hubby to see me climax. Wow! That was quite a day. The Holy Spirit gave me a whole new outlook on sexual play in that one simple blog post. With my newly gained freedom, our lovemaking became really great! We feel so close to each other now.

Thanks for walking me through this touchy subject. We hope our story will help other couples.

Free and loving it.

In this letter we see both the joy and the controversy of sexual freedom within the context of marriage. Nothing in life is more enjoyable than lovers frolicking in the safest of all playgrounds. Its protective boundary is the unchanging covenant between one man, one woman, and the one true God. There is no freer place to be. Yet within its borders remain decisions that must be made. What are the limits of the sexual liberty we've received in marriage?

Joys and Controversies of Sexual Freedom

In the garden of Eden, Adam and Eve were "free to eat of any tree in the garden." Yet there was one tree whose fruit they "must not eat" (Genesis 3:16–17). In the beginning God provided freedom to Adam and Eve, but freedom in the context of healthy boundaries. The same principle applies to sexual freedom. God has given us a "garden" to fully enjoy. But are there limitations to sexual freedom? Of course there are. Are we required to do everything our partner desires? No, we are not.

Playground rules are needed to ensure the safety and enjoyment for both husband and wife. Liberty enhances shared pleasure in marriage. However, we should say no to anything that is:

- Involuntary—partners need to agree.
- Painful—seek pleasure, not pain.
- Bondage—physical restraint is dark.
- Dangerous—e.g. anal sex can cause serious injury.
- Demeaning—your spouse is a child of the King.
- Frightening—the playground must feel safe and secure.
- Offensive—respect your mate's conscience.
- Public—sexual intimacy must always be private.

First Corinthians 8:9 makes it clear: "Be careful, however, that the exercise of your freedom does not become a stumbling block." Although the apostle Paul was referring to freedom in the context of what Jewish believers should or should not eat, we believe this principle also applies to sexual liberty within marriage. Our friend Dr. Wayne Inzer states this very succinctly when he says, "My freedom should never be a weapon or instrument of harm to my partner."[1]

It is common in the church for both husbands and wives to have concerns about oral sex. At some of our Schools of Supernatural Marriage, half of the questions have been about this subject. For this reason, we have chosen it to begin our discussion on freedom.

Those who are accepting of oral sexual stimulation find it to be an enjoyable and effective way to bring pleasure to their partner. For many husbands and wives, it is a powerful method for arousing the one they love and helping them to achieve orgasm. Others are concerned about oral sex because a husband spilling "his semen on the ground" might prevent pregnancy and be offensive to God. This apprehension usually stems from the following passage about Onan, Judah's son:

> Then Judah said to Onan, "Lie with your brother's wife [Tamar] and fulfill your duty to her as a brother-in-law to produce offspring for your brother." But Onan knew that the offspring would not be his; so whenever he lay with his brother's wife, he spilled his semen on the ground to keep from producing offspring for his brother. What he did was wicked in the LORD's sight; so he put him to death also (Genesis 38:8–10).

1   Robert Wayne Inzer, M.D., F.A.C.O.G., Residency Program Director, Department of Obstetrics and Gynecology, Baylor University Medical Center; Professor of Medicine, Baylor University Medical Center; and Assistant Professor of Medicine, Texas A&M School of Medicine.

Although there are differences of opinion on what this and many other Scriptures mean, we believe Onan's offense was not simply that "he spilled his semen on the ground." Rather, his unwillingness to fulfill the obligation of continuing his brother's bloodline was the sin of rebellion. The patriarch Judah, societal norms of the day, and apparently God Himself required that this be done. It is our understanding that this passage has much to say about direct rebellion against God and has little connection to concerns about oral sex within marriage.

This controversy, however, can be a major challenge for some couples to overcome. It is much like the question of "eating food sacrificed to idols" Paul addresses in 1 Corinthians 8. Clearly, Paul understood that eating this food was not, in itself, a sin. Yet he advised that those who felt defiled by the food would be sinning if they ate what was sacrificed to idols. His point was that no one should break his or her conscience on such an issue. And we completely agree.

We believe the use of oral sex in the lovemaking of marriage is not a matter of sin, but is one of conscience, which we'll discuss further in a later chapter. God's truths are eternal, which means they never change. But our understanding and opinions often transition over time.

If there is disparity as to what husband and wife believe on this issue, both need to press into the Holy Spirit to discern wise council in the matter. The Holy Spirit is in the center of every supernatural marriage. If we listen well, He will lead us exactly where we should go. Wherever the Spirit leads us in intimacy, we are blessed.

God Wants Us to Be Free

God really wants us to be free to enjoy sexual play in marriage. He is a good God who created a good thing when He invented sex.

> *Optimizing freedom is a great way to maximize the enjoyment of play in the marriage bed.*

Let's start at the beginning to discover God's plan for sexual intimacy by looking at Genesis 2:16–18, 22, and 24–25.

And the LORD God commanded the man, "You are *free to eat from any tree in the garden*; but you must *not eat* from the tree of the knowledge of good and evil, for when you eat of it you will surely die."

The LORD God said, "It is not good for the man to be alone. I will make him a helper suitable for him."

…Then the LORD *God made a woman* from the rib he had taken out of the man, *and he brought her to the man.*

For this reason a man will leave his father and mother and be united to his wife, and they will *become one flesh*.

The man and his wife were both *naked*, and they *felt no shame*.

The garden of Eden was created to be the safest and best of all playgrounds. Adam and Eve were "free to eat from any tree in the garden." It was all "dos" and only one "don't." The boundary set in place for their protection was to "not eat" from only one tree while enjoying all the other trees there. God gives us similar liberty in the sexual playground of marriage. It is good for husbands and wives to personally experience the pleasant intimacies we are designed to enjoy with each other.

"God made a woman…and he brought her to the man." Adam and Eve were introduced relationally so that they would come together sexually and "become one flesh." Freedom reigned in the garden of Eden. God blessed Adam and Eve through His joyful command to "Prosper! Reproduce! Fill Earth!" (Genesis 1:28, MSG). It was a pleasant task to satisfy His demand. They both were naked yet "felt no shame" from their sexual freedom. And neither should we. Taking physical pleasure in one another was a charge Adam and Eve were happy to obey. And God's design for perfect marriage has not changed since that time.

Genesis 1:28 reminds us of a story of a census taker who was going house to house throughout a neighborhood. He came to one house, knocked on the door, and a woman answered. He asked, "How many children do you have and what are their ages?"

She answered, "Well, let's see. We have Jenny and Benny. They're ten years old. We have Lonnie and Johnnie. They're twelve. We have Timmy and Jimmy. They're—"

The census taker interrupted, "Hold on! You mean to tell me that you got twins every time?"

"Absolutely not," she replied. "There were hundreds of times we didn't get anything."[2]

We believe God wants your sex life to be outrageously wonderful. He created your sexual responses to be passionate, unpredictable, and amazingly strong. To reach the highest levels of sexual expression, both you and your partner must be free. Ask God to make you an extravagant lover, experiencing intimacy beyond what you have known. His response will exceed your imagination.

The Song of Solomon expresses many ideas that can expand your freedom in lovemaking. Consider this passage with your mind wide open:

> Behold, thou art fair, my beloved, yea, pleasant:
> Also our bed is green.
> The beams of our house are cedar,
> And our rafters of fir
> (Song of Solomon 1:16–17, KJV).

Grass is green. Cedars and firs grow in the forest. The message of this Scripture is pretty clear:

Find a very safe place where you and your spouse can enjoy the great outdoors in a way you will never forget!

---

2 Jan Karon, *In the Company of Others: A Father Tim Novel* (New York: Penguin Group, 2011), 208.

King Solomon would encourage you to try this. And so do we.

There are beautiful thoughts on being free in the New Testament as well. Jesus said, "If the Son sets you free, you will be free indeed" (John 8:36). This includes freedom in marriage. And Paul's declarations about freedom apply to every aspect of life together in marriage—sexual pleasure included: "Now the Lord is the Spirit, and where the Spirit of the Lord is, there is freedom" (2 Corinthians 3:17).

Getting Free

God placed in us the desire to live and love freely. We believe three things are needed if we are to step into the sexual liberty God planned for us to enjoy: lordship, deliverance, and transformation. The Holy Spirit provides our access to each of these. And it is this same Spirit who sustains them in our lives. Let's look at the keys to getting free.

Lordship is the clear message of Exodus 20:3, the first of the Ten Commandments, "You shall have no other gods before me." When we are properly aligned with God as our top priority, everything else seems to fall into place. I (Linda) discovered this the hard way a few years ago.

One Sunday morning at church, I had a glimpse of the pure and holy jealousy of God. Although constantly busy with church activities and Bible classes for women and children in our community, God revealed to me that I had allowed pleasing Dan to take a higher place in my heart than pleasing Him. Our marriage had become my idol.

Faced with this choice of lordship, I wrestled with God for three days. I loved our marriage and was afraid that it might change if I repented. Satan is such a mean liar. Ha! It did change, but only for the better! Dan and I were both now free to love God with all our hearts. Our relationship became richer and more fulfilling as proper lordship was reestablished.

Interestingly, years later I was reading about the woman who kissed Jesus' feet in Luke 7. I told Jesus that I wanted to kiss His feet and He seemed very pleased with the idea. As I began visualizing kissing His feet, I noticed that they looked like Dan's. Curious about this, I asked Jesus what it meant. He replied that it is all a matter of my heart. When I love or serve Jesus, it is often demonstrated in how I love and serve Dan. In my heart I must have loving Jesus as my priority. Dan often gets to be the happy recipient as I pour my love out to Jesus.

Lordship is the key that unlocks the door to freedom. But it is *deliverance* that then pushes the door open. On one hand, we know that God truly wants His children to be free. On the other hand, it is clear that satan is hell-bent on sentencing us all to life in prison. He holds us back in our ability to love with the chains of trauma, unforgiveness, fear, and sin—the very things that restrain us in relationships, in worship, and in play. But we are far from defeated. Deliverance is at hand!

> Jesus is the deliverer who breaks open the door
> of our personal prisons and sets us free.
> The Holy Spirit then empowers us to walk into
> freedom with the Lord at our head.

He gives us an abundant life that is filled with satisfaction, peace, and joyful expectation of what is yet to come. We receive liberty that changes how we live and how we love.

An acquaintance of ours was trapped for years in a lifestyle built around drug addiction, which she paid for through her daily work in prostitution. From the perspective of the world, there was no hope for her to lead a normal and productive life. A woman from our church believed differently and pursued Susan with love and truth straight from the heart of God.

Within months, Susan committed her life to Jesus and asked Him to break through the gate holding her captive. As He led the way to freedom, she was wise enough to follow. The Holy Spirit transformed Susan's mind and brought healing to her heart. She was delivered from drug addiction and left her life on the street to become healthy, whole, and powerful in the kingdom of light. Her life and successful marriage are testimonies to the goodness of God. Her story brings hope to those in the direst of needs.

The truth is that our lives have much in common with what Susan experienced. All of us have been imprisoned by lies and deceptions that are birthed within the kingdom of darkness. Each of us has suffered bondage. Our chains may have had different names from those that imprisoned Susan, but our captivity was no less severe. It is only through the intervention of Jesus as our deliverer that any of us receive liberty. Christ sets us free to be the men and women, husbands and wives, we were created to be—living and loving without restraint.

Our personal story of advancing in freedom began when trusted friends spent some hours with us in focused prayer. To our surprise, we became better lovers! Our love level deepened and we found a new joy in lovemaking. It became so simple to just enjoy one another in the safe playground of our bedroom. Suddenly, we became free to love and be vulnerable with others in sharing what God has given to us. We write of this time in *7 Secrets of a Supernatural Marriage*:

Several years ago, Linda went through an afternoon of teaching and prayer focused on deliverance. The Holy Spirit brought to her mind events from childhood that had never really been dealt with or healed. She was enabled to forgive every hurt the Holy Spirit brought to her mind and repent for participating in things that were not of God. Linda was freed from the control of fear of man and also from pride. That night she felt a deep sense of inner peace and an increased level of confidence that she had never sensed before. No doubt about it—something of great significance had occurred within her during the events of the afternoon!

Linda had always been a gentle person who possessed the ability to love people deeply. Following her time in prayer ministry, I (Dan) could sense that the intensity of the love she shared had entered a new and higher level. She had loved me deeply for years, but suddenly she loved me even more than before. There was a change within her that was hard to explain. Even our sexual intimacy improved dramatically.

I wasn't surprised that Linda had been blessed through her prayer experience, as most people feel a deep sense of joy and peace for a time after intense communion with God. I purposefully watched her week after week to see how long the spiritual high would last. To my amazement, even after months it did not wear off. She was permanently changed by God's power and presence. We both liked it![3]

When freed through deliverance, *transformation* soon follows. As we receive the mind of Christ (1 Corinthians 2:16), our patterns of thinking learned from the kingdom of darkness are transformed to match the very thoughts of heaven. Our habits of living then flow from the revelation of who we are in Christ and how we can best show love to our neighbor. And there is no closer neighbor than the one we marry.

I (Dan) was delivered from deeply-rooted anger in 2006. But the default setting of my life remained leaning toward becoming angry when my expectations were not met. It took several more years for the peace of Christ to transform my entrenched relational habits. But our marriage immediately improved after my deliverance. It has been a joy for both

3   Dan and Linda Wilson, *7 Secrets of a Supernatural Marriage: The Joy of Spirit-Led Intimacy* (Racine, WI: Broadstreet Publishing, 2014), 77–78.

Linda and me to watch God gradually replace my tradition of angry responses with the fruit of His Spirit.

The very Spirit of God changes us from the inside out. We are transformed as He pours fruit into our hearts: love, joy, peace, patience, kindness, goodness, faithfulness, gentleness, and self-control (Galatians 5:22–23). These are essential traits for those who would become the greatest lovers on earth. We cannot acquire even one of them through study or human effort; they are given to us by the Spirit as we love God first and walk in His glorious freedom.

Staying Free

The fruit of the Spirit that blesses our lovemaking also confirms that great battles have been won. Yet it is never wise to rest on the laurels of victory. Though our enemy is defeated, he accepts no truce. He strives daily to regain all lost ground. Our freedom is precious and worth the fight. And there are actually times when making love shifts the war.

Christy and Carl had a great marriage. They truly loved each other, and they both loved the Lord. Carl was a dentist with a thriving practice. He was a leader in their church and coached their son's soccer team. He was a busy man. Christy enjoyed being a wife and mom. She volunteered at the kids' elementary school, she led a women's Bible study in their home, and many women looked to her for advice and counsel. Some days she found that she did not enjoy even a moment of quiet.

With their hectic schedules, communication was not always the best. Fatigue would hit them from time to time, and occasionally one would snap at the other. Disunity would attempt to rear its ugly head. Sometimes they became so angry at each other that they seemed to be enemies instead of allies.

Christy and Carl made a brilliant discovery: sex is a unifier. They knew the enemy would want to divide them, bringing discord and discouragement. God used sex to unite them, restoring harmony and peace between the two. They discovered that He designed sex as a marvelous weapon to be used in the war of good versus evil, of unity versus disunity. Nothing restored their relationship more quickly or more satisfyingly than sex. Like Christy and Carl, you too can be freedom fighters! Through sex at the right time, in the right attitude, and in the right way, you can make both love *and* war!

Paul tells us in Romans 16:19–20 to be "wise about what is good, and innocent about what is evil. The God of peace will soon crush satan under your feet." At times, together, you can wisely choose sex (something good) as a weapon to fight what is evil. Physically uniting can increase your oneness with each other and with God.

> *Strong marriages are satan's worst nightmare, and united you will defeat the attack from the enemy.*

Enjoy Your Freedom

Worshiping together is a pleasant and powerful way to fight the enemy too. We love to worship regularly with our brothers and sisters at church, but our favorite time to worship is at home with our iPod playing a great list of our favorite worship songs. We sing along. We dance a little. Sometimes we sit, while at other times we lie down. Often we pray for each other. And the Holy Spirit always comes and touches us.

There is nothing quite like being deeply loved by God and each other in the peaceful setting of our home. The harmony and unity between the three of us is precious—husband, wife, and God together as one. This truly is holy matrimony.

It has been our experience that after worshiping together like this, we feel extremely intimate. Our entire beings—mind, body, and spirit—are in alignment. Quite naturally, we desire each other physically. And, beautifully, we are aware that the Holy Spirit is right there with us.

God enjoys us enjoying each other.

Once a pastor in Uganda told us he and his wife experienced this same desire for sex after worshiping and praying together. Since then we have discovered that it is common in strong, godly marriages. There are two ground rules that we follow, and we recommend that you have similar boundaries as the Spirit leads.

Our first ground rule is that we *never* initiate a time of worship with the goal of its leading to romance. And the second is that we always complete our planned time of worship before transitioning into play. However, we believe that lovemaking is a form of worship. It is healthy and good to commune with God, who is love, while taking pleasure in our love for one another.

As God spoke to Joshua, He would still say to us today: "I will never leave you nor forsake you" (Joshua 1:5). The promise of His presence is assured every moment of our lives, including the most intimate of times in marriage. The intense physical oneness that husbands and wives enjoy together flows from the wellspring of union that is God Himself.

Jesus prayed for oneness:

> My prayer is not for them alone. I pray also for those who will believe in me through their message, that all of them may be one, Father, just as you are in me and I am in you. May they also be in us so that the world may believe that you have sent me. I have given them the glory that you gave me, that they may be one as we are one: I in them and you in me. May they be brought to complete unity to let the world know that you sent me and have loved them even as you have loved me (John 17:20–23).

The triune God—Father, Spirit, and Son—possesses a degree of unity we long to comprehend. In this prayer, Jesus speaks His yearning "that they may be one as we are one." In marriage, we find the ultimate opportunity to satisfy His prayer. Sexual union celebrates the intense oneness intended for man, woman, and God. When one with Him, we are drawn closer to each other; conversely, as we are one with each other, we're drawn closer to Him. The intimacy of heaven can manifest delightfully in marriage on earth.

True intimacy with God improves every aspect of our intimacy in marriage. He blesses our oneness, including our "one flesh" relations, when we pursue Him. The pleasure of husband and wife joining together in body is enhanced by the presence of the Spirit—God's seal of approval of their union.

We know that "where the Spirit of the Lord is, there is freedom" (2 Corinthians 3:17). It is wise for husbands and wives to invite the Holy Spirit into the center of their marriage relationships, including the times they become physically one. Liberty in sexual expression is a vital part of being "free indeed" (John 8:36).

DR. DAN'S PRESCRIPTIONS FOR LIBERATE

* Greet your husband at the door wearing nothing but one of his shirts.
* Take turns coaxing each other into a new location, position, rhythm, or time for play.
* Apply whipped cream to various body parts. Remove only using lips and tongue.

3

Communicate

Patrick blurted out that his wife rarely touched him. His pain was clearly visible. "But every time I touch him," shot back Chrissy, "he thinks I want sex!" Clearly this precious couple desired a little help in navigating these troubled marital waters.

Chrissy knew that her hubby wanted and needed touch, and even needed sexual touch. Patrick's response was much like that of many men. His father had abandoned him at a young age. Sexual touch made him feel loved, safe, and secure. He needed her. And he needed her touch.

Touch does not always indicate a desire for sex. Chrissy and Patrick suffered from classic miscommunication. At first Chrissy balked at our counsel, but she agreed to try it. We advised a new bedtime routine.

Before attempting sleep, Patrick and Chrissy now hop into bed and cuddle. Eventually they assume the nesting spoons position with each lying on their side, her bottom nestled against his tummy. This feels safe and secure. Now here is the fun part—Chrissy reaches back, holding Patrick's penis in her hand while at the same time Patrick reaches forward holding her breast. Ahhhh.

Patrick laughs that the first several nights of following our advice he was so excited it took an hour to go to sleep. Now they love it! He gets his need for touch fulfilled. She feels safe and is unafraid of him demanding sex each night. Both of them are feeling loved. Both are relaxed and sleeping well. They are freely discussing needs and freely using touch as a way of communicating love and security. And *sometimes* the touch escalates when they are not quite so sleepy yet.

Communication is a core value of every healthy marriage relationship. Think of it as a life-giving connection between the minds, hearts, and bodies of husband and wife. Without valid communication, a man and woman only *live together*. But with it they have the awesome opportunity to *commune (join) together* in intense oneness that is beyond comprehension.

> *If husband and wife desire to exuberantly enjoy their sexual relationship, they must communicate well and often.*

Honestly, some subjects are more fun to talk about than others. But one thing is for sure: sex can be an enticing topic of discussion between two mates. Romantic thoughts that are spoken and heard well can be a delight. But there are times that intimate messages are best shared without words.

Talk without Words

The story of Patrick and Chrissy is a wonderful demonstration of how a couple can use nonverbal means to communicate thoughts of great significance to one another each night as they prepare for sleep. Their new bedtime pattern is much more than a habit or mindless routine. It is a creative and pleasant example of how partners can have a joyful love-talk in the midst of blissful silence. Actions like these can speak louder than words, expressing marriage-building sentiments:

- Love
- Acceptance
- Warmth
- Sexual attraction and appreciation
- Desire for oneness, even when not sexually aroused
- Interest in further lovemaking when the right time comes

When used well, sex is the ultimate form of nonverbal communication—a two-way encounter that brings depth and richness to the bond of marriage.

God's plan is that lovemaking be a rich and satisfying experience for both husband and wife. Spouses give and receive intense communication of love that is expressed through the most personal of human languages.

What nonverbal steps can lovers take that set the stage for sex to speak in the most gratifying way? What will make the conversation most delightful? Let us make a few practical suggestions.

Proximity: Making an effort to be in the same room together is a way of saying, "I want to be near you." Relational intimacy, the ideal ambiance for lovemaking, is much more difficult to maintain from afar. There are seasons when physical separation is unavoidable, but wisdom would encourage couples to be within talking and touching range as often as possible. Ask God for creativity to plan ways that you can physically be with the one you love. In fact, when is the last time your wife sat in your lap, hubby? She is much more interesting than a football game on TV.

Time: Quality time together, particularly with the two of you alone, is fertile soil for the growth of sexual desire. It is irreplaceable. If your lifestyle does not allow you to share the precious substance of time with your lover, the lifestyle *needs* to change.

Eye contact: They say a picture is worth a thousand words. Do you remember catching your mate's eyes the first time you saw them? A moment of intentional, sustained eye contact between a woman and a man can be worth a myriad of words. Many people remember catching each other's eyes as an unforgettable first step toward desiring to be a couple. The Holy Spirit often uses this method of imprinting in His matchmaking. It is said that "the eyes are the window to the soul."[1] Certainly, eyes give many clues as to what is going on in the soul—the mind, will, and emotions.[2]

---

1   This is an Old English proverb stemming from Matthew 6:22–23.
2   For a further discussion of the soul, see our book *7 Secrets of a Supernatural Marriage*, pages 95, 98–100.

Gazing game: Right now (or as soon as possible), grab your mate and convince him or her that you would like to play a little game. This is going to be fun! Stand face-to-face, about two to three feet apart, gazing directly into each other's eyes. No touching! Take turns wordlessly expressing the following thoughts to one another. Yes, you may do this as many times as you wish. But please note that, as the authors, we are not responsible for what happens at the end of the exercise.

- I enjoy looking at you.
- You are fun to be with.
- I love you.
- I am attracted to you.
- I desire to be intimate with you.

Casual touch: In the healthiest of marriage relationships, touch becomes a normal part of everyday life. We are all born with inner needs both to touch and to be touched. We are all aware that this is true of infants and small children. The opportunities for touch become less frequent when we become adults. Yet God placed this need for touch deep within, and it will remain for a lifetime.

Years ago we began the habit of briefly touching one another often when we are together. This can be as small as a brief touch on the shoulder while walking through the kitchen, or it can be a big hug with a peck on the cheek just to say, "You are loved." Casual touch is intended to be non-demanding. There are no strings attached. It is an important foundational element for a love relationship that lasts.

Intimate touch: This kind of body contact tends to be firmer, closer, longer touches than the casual type we have just described. Pressure or stroking is applied close to or on *erogenous* areas that would normally not be touched in public. (Note that words in bold italics are defined more completely in the glossary at the back of this book.)

It is purposeful flirtation with intent to express a desire for sexual play. As its intensity escalates, sexual touch can communicate an urgent desire or need to have an overtly sexual encounter.

The ultimate purpose of sexual touch, as with all forms of nonverbal communication in marriage, is for both husband and wife to convey to their partner the consistent and unforgettable message that they are *loved*. There are no limitations as to how and how often this can be expressed. But don't rely on sex alone to say, "I love you." You must use your God-given imagination to share this thought with your mate in as many ways as possible. There are times it might even be best to use words.

A Time to Speak

In Ecclesiastes, King Solomon wrote there is "a time to keep silence, and a time to speak (3:7, NKJV). Just as you passionately speak words of love and commitment to God, the covenant of marriage requires that you do the same with your spouse. In marriage you have the opportunity to share stresses, victories, and disappointments with your mate, the one you have chosen to love for a lifetime.

What a privilege it is to speak. Are you listening, men? Your innermost thoughts are often best shared with your mate using actual *words*. Allowing emotion to show as the words are spoken will only increase their power, not hinder it. Thoughts that are not communicated may have little direct impact on your partner.

Sexual satisfaction is enhanced when physical intimacy is accompanied by words that are well used.

When teaching about communication in marriage, we sometimes use a ball to symbolize spoken words. The person holding the ball gets to be the one talking. The goal is that speaking to one another would bring spouses as much pleasure as two children enjoy while playing catch on a lazy summer day. One child carefully and purposefully throws the ball (the spoken word) so that the other can gleefully catch it. This is not dodge ball we are playing here. There is never a desire to do harm; playing together with shear delight is the intention of the day. And have you noticed that *both* kids throw and catch the ball? A game of catch isn't very fun if one person holds the ball without throwing it, nor is it fun if one person refuses to catch the ball tossed to him or her.

Use words to have fun! Flirt with your words. Kindly tease each other. What words might be spoken to enhance the atmosphere of childlike playfulness in your marriage? Paul gives us a hint when he writes to the Philippians, "Whatever is true, whatever is noble, whatever is right, whatever is pure, whatever is lovely, whatever is admirable—if anything is excellent or praiseworthy—think about such things" (4:8). It is crucial that husbands and wives not only *think* about things that are true, noble, pure, and admirable, but also *say* them to their mate. Wise lovers put their thoughts into action through speaking gentle and affirming words.

It is healthy for lovers to discuss lovemaking. As you talk about adapting to each other's sexual opinions and desires, sensitivity is required. Sex is a delicate and vulnerable subject. The following *be–attitudes* will help you communicate sexually with pleasure and honor:

- Be willing to *listen*, *consider*, and *speak*.
- Be willing to *not force* your partner.
- Be willing to *try things* your partner desires.
- Be willing to *say no*, gently and lovingly.
- Be willing to *accept a no*. Freedom goes both ways.

> Your mission, should you choose to accept it,
> is to use words to destroy every blockade that
> would interfere with good sex.

Throw words that are right, lovely, excellent, and praiseworthy to your partner. When you put this into practice, be assured that "the God of peace will be with you" (Philippians 4:9). He is the One who destroys the barriers to intimacy within marriage. Expressing these uplifting thoughts sets the stage for the two of you to become best friends and satisfied lovers forever.

A Time to Listen

I (Linda) want to share how learning to talk and listen well blessed the friendship and intimacy in my marriage with Dan. Even though I might be a bit quieter than some women, I still love to talk. And more to the point, I desire to be heard. This is especially true when it comes to Dan—and even more so when our sons were young.

I loved being a stay-at-home mom with our boys. But by the end of the day I was often desperate for someone to talk to. An adult. And not just any adult. I wanted Dan. All I needed was a short talk with him, and I could be a happy camper once again.

But there were two sides to this story. Dan had a very busy medical practice. From early each morning until early in the evening he would be caring for people. He worked hard—all day, every day. Dan craved silence. He longed to simply lie down on the couch with a newspaper for a few minutes upon arriving home. Not much to ask, right? But it felt like I might explode if I didn't get some words out. I needed some empathy, some understanding from my lover, my friend. Talking with a newspaper between us was maddening.

So how did we resolve this communication dilemma? The Holy Spirit showed Dan that if he could delay his need for rest and quiet just a few minutes, giving me his undivided attention, I could quickly tell him about my day. Then I would be his contented wife once again. Simple? Yes. But it was a great sacrifice from my hardworking husband. This became our new, normal routine. All of this communicated Dan's love for me, and it showed me day after day that he valued me. Me. Dan valued *me*.

Now what might this story have to do with lovemaking? Everything. Feeling valued makes me feel sexy. It reminds me that I am desirable. And that, my friends, puts a spring in my step and a song in my heart. I love it when my lover listens to me.

Much can be learned about your spouse when you not only listen with your ears, but also hear with your heart. And knowing every detail about one another is a catalyst for excellent lovemaking. A simple instruction that builds relational strength in marriage is to speak clearly, but focus more on careful listening. Active listening is just as important as what is spoken if good communication is to occur.

*Time spent listening to the thoughts and
the dreams of the one you love is always worthwhile.*

Talk to each other *a lot*. This is just as important after thirty years of marriage as it is during courtship. Couples never outgrow the need to share their dreams and consider how they might someday step into them together. Plan for the future with the one you love. Reminisce about great memories from the past. Express emotions such as sadness or joy. Be silly!

Talking with your partner about *lovemaking*—before, during, and after your intimate encounters—can be so much fun! Although it is possible for conversation to become overly focused on sex, it is more common that couples do not discuss the topic enough. In marriage there are no limitations as to what can be discussed concerning this exciting subject. It is a laudable goal for wives and husbands to discuss every detail of their sexual relationship together. The more you know of each other's desires and needs, the better equipped you will be to satisfy one another.

As you share every aspect of life with your mate, focus on communicating the things that really matter. The primary messages that your partner needs to hear from your heart are:

- I love you.
- I am committed to you.
- I am available for you.

Envision a three-legged stool. You want it to be strong so you can rest on it without fear of it collapsing. These messages are the three legs that provide support for relational stability in marriage. When all three are understood, your lover will know you are worthy of trust. The two of you will be able to handle the pressures of daily living, and will be able to give and receive the intimacies of making love.

David and Melissa had a wonderful, stable marriage relationship. Love, commitment, and availability were all firmly in place. A situation suddenly came up one day that needed to be resolved. But could she talk about it? And would he be willing to listen?

"To shave or not to shave?" That was the question posed

one day when Melissa read a magazine article while waiting for her haircut. The article described Brazilian shaves in which all the woman's pubic hair is trimmed away. It stated that the sensations for both the woman and the man during intercourse were different after shaving. The article even claimed that it was sexy for the man to shave his wife. Melissa was not excited about this idea, but she was willing to try just about anything that had potential to please her man. She wanted to ask her husband, but wondered, "Can I even mention something as embarrassing as this?"

Tentatively, she told David what she had read. Her husband had never heard of Brazilian shaves before. David was quick to tell Melissa that he was perfectly happy with her as she was, but that she was free to shave if she wanted. *Only* if she wanted! He went on to tell her how great it made him feel that she desired to be an adventurous lover talking about such things with him. He was pleased that she had asked. And she was pleased that he had left the ball in her court. Her question answered, Melissa began the plan for their next romantic adventure.

The Holy Spirit is astonishingly wise and has the answer to every embarrassing question you may have. He knows what is best for you and your mate. God wants you both to be the greatest of lovers, and He is willing to lead you where you need to go. If you are listening, He will lead you as a couple into what is joyful, exciting, satisfying, and fun! There is no fear in talking about, dreaming about, or enjoying anything within the safe playground of marriage.

Mission: Possible

Openly discussing sex with your mate is not Mission: Impossible. You can do it! Knowing what your partner thinks, feels, and believes is truly important. Ask him or her what feels really good. Tell your partner what you find to be delightful. Help each other to know what to do and what to avoid in optimizing arousal and pleasure.

> *Talking about sex is a wonderful opportunity*
> *to increase your level of enjoyment.*

If it is difficult at first to talk in the midst of lovemaking, remember the value of nonverbal communication. Guide your partner's hands and fingers to touch you where it feels the best. Show them motions that cause you to be aroused. Release moans of contentment and sounds of excitement as they bring you to a higher plane.

When you are able, progress to verbal hints, and then on to clear directives using specific words to describe what you enjoy the most. Gracefully accept being told to try something different. Bodies change every day, and what worked well tonight might be less than exciting tomorrow. The better you know one another's intimate desires, the more effective you will be as lovers.

While involved in sex with your mate, remember to say words that will build them up and strengthen the bond between the two of you. Whisper to them how deeply they are loved. Compliment your spouse's body and celebrate the parts you enjoy the most. Thank him or her for making it their desire to satisfy yours. Rejoice with them in the peace and contentment you share.

All dialogue between lovers is important, whether or not words are used. Kindness shown in the kitchen Friday night can lead to a Sunday afternoon filled with delight. Your goal in marriage is expressing true love to your partner in every way it can be received. God has poured *His love* into your heart by the Holy Spirit (Romans 5:5) so that you and your mate can share this love together. Forever.

DR. DAN'S PRESCRIPTIONS FOR COMMUNICATE

* Send your mate a suggestive text today. Learn from the mistakes of others and be sure it goes to the correct phone number.
* Write love notes to each other. Leave them in unexpected places, such as your bathroom mirror, car, or a napkin in the lunchbox.
* Ask the Holy Spirit to give you positive words that you can speak to bless and build up your mate.

4
Entice

Diane frequently complained that her husband, Steve, was not romantic. He was great with conversation; he was a fun companion. And he was even a good cook. But there was a serious deficit in his romancing. Both Diane and Steve expressed desire for more frequent lovemaking. Steve was into the sexual play: slam, bam, done. Diane, however, desired enticement—a gradual build-up toward a sexual encounter.

One afternoon Diane approached us bubbling over with excitement. On the previous day she had experienced a rough day at work. Upon arriving home, she was greeted with nice music, delicious aromas of dinner simmering on the stove, and she was surprised to find sticky notes all over the house. Steve had placed notes on light switches, on the bathroom mirror, and on the refrigerator door. Each note said something loving and romantic. She was thrilled by the effort her sweet husband had gone to on her behalf. She felt loved. She felt desired. She felt hungry for Steve.

Entice Is a Verb

Entice. Attract. Coax. Seduce. These synonyms paint the picture of a husband or wife offering sexual pleasure to their lover, artfully arousing desire in their mate. Enticement in godly marriage is much deeper than mere sexual allurement.

> *Enticement combines the excitement*
> *of persuasion toward intimacy with the*
> *mystery and love of gentle romance.*

The meanings of the verbs *entice* and *romance* are so complexly intertwined that we will use them interchangeably in the pages to come. Verbs imply *action!* Entice your mate into an active love relationship that is intensely satisfying. Enjoy fanning the flames of desire within your marriage by attracting and coaxing one another into lovemaking. Good sex is good for *both* of you.

Ask the Spirit to awaken the craving for intimacy that God placed within you. Then shift internal thoughts and feelings outwardly into words and actions. Act out the desire to be one flesh with the one you love, enticing your mate into a flourishing love relationship.

During courtship, the feeling of love and the sense of sexual attraction lead couples to consider joining together for a lifetime in marriage. It is important for both love and attraction between spouses to continue deepening through the years. As with a fine red wine, the value of romantic enticement in marriage only increases with time.

God shows us the treasure of enticement in a love relationship through His amazing prevenient grace. "What in the world is that?" you may be asking. Well, actually it is not of the world; it is otherworldly. It is supernatural. And what could it possibly have to do with romance? Everything.

We learned about *prevenient grace* from some Methodist friends on a Walk to Emmaus retreat. This particular aspect of grace is that in which God's amazing grace toward us precedes our desire for Him. The Holy Spirit draws us, pursues us, and woos us into relationship with the Lord. John expresses it this way in one of his letters, "We love Him because He first loved us" (1 John 4:19, NKJV).

This enticement from God was spoken of three thousand years ago when King Solomon painted a beautiful picture of romance using the paintbrush of poetry.

> You have stolen my heart, my sister, my bride;
> you have stolen my heart
> with one glance of your eyes,
> with one jewel of your necklace.
> How delightful is your love, my sister, my bride!
> How much more pleasing is your love than wine,
> and the fragrance of your perfume than any spice!
> (Song of Solomon 4:9–10)

Isn't this the way enticing your lover works? One of you is feeling romantic, so you begin enticing, romancing, and wooing your mate toward a love encounter. Holy God is the Lover teaching us how to love. And, as we keep on saying, holy really is fun! Keeping this special form of grace in mind, let's explore the stages of enticement in marriage.

Increasing Enticement

Gaze: Solomon wrote in the fourth chapter of his Song that a glance of the eyes can be a dramatic entrance to romantic encounter. Without a sound, gazing can say, "You have caught my attention. I notice you. You are attractive to me." And the message will be clearly heard.

If the eyes truly are the window to the soul, an intense gaze between two lovers' eyes can fling the window wide open. Romance can begin with a glance, escalating quickly as the gaze is maintained.

It is not surprising that the eyes have a profound influence on our thoughts. The average person has 2.5 million nerve fibers carrying visual information from their two eyes to their brain. This massive input of data takes up 30 percent of the entire computing capacity of the brain[1]—compared to just 8 percent for touch and only 3 percent for hearing.[2] Since we use *all* of our senses in lovemaking, unquestionably, our eyes play a major role.

> *Sexual enticement for both women and men*
> *is profoundly influenced by what we see.*

---

1   Josr B. Jonas, Andreas M. Schmidt, Jens A. Muller-Bergh, Ursula M. Schldrzer-Schrehardr, and Gottfried O. H. Naumann, "Human Optic Nerve Fiber Count and Optic Disc Size," *Investigative Ophthalmology & Visual Science*, Vol. 33, No. 6, May 1992, Copyright © Association for Research in Vision and Ophthalmology.

2   Denise Grady, "The Vision Thing: Mainly in the Brain," from the June 1993 issue of *Discover Magazine*, www.discovermagazine.com/1993/jun /thevisionthingma227.

Some are more focused on the appearance of clothes that are worn or the cleanliness and beauty of a bedroom. Others pay particular attention to the contours of their lover or are fascinated by looking at their favorite body parts. Both genders are drawn toward lovemaking by what they see.

The eye gate plays a powerful role in attraction and bonding between you and your mate. Gaze is not meant for lusting after others outside of marriage or leading you into an adulterous relationship with pictures on a screen. Your eyes were created to focus exclusively on the one you have promised to love for life. A glance of the eyes can light the fire of romance through *all* the years of marriage.

Flirt: Flirtation ramps things up to a higher level of mutual enticement. Couples use the eyes to give and receive *the look* that both of them understand. But there are many kinds of flirts lovers might use that are joyful, exciting, and fun. The key is to keep childhood playfulness in the midst of this enjoyable adult game.

It is really fun learning how to be more childlike from our grandchildren. Our young grandson is thoroughly "in the moment." When he sees Ninja Turtles, he is completely engrossed in them. He loves his *Star Wars* book, fully engaged with the characters while looking at the pictures. Be it sports or cartoons, he enthusiastically participates in whatever he is engaged in. Can that be said of us in our pursuit of our spouse?

Are you fully "in the moment" with your mate while enticing them to love, or is the to-do list popping in and out of your thoughts? Women seem to struggle with this more than men. Females see the piles of laundry, the stacks of dishes, with thoughts flitting in and out of their brains in rapid-fire succession. Men, on the other hand, can seemingly dismiss all thoughts other than the pursuit and enticement of their wives for lovemaking. Engaging your mind in sexual play will surely make you a better and more satisfied lover.

Perhaps it's time to increase variety in flirting.

One idea we propose is a simple Facebook post expressing love—especially on a day when it is *not* expected like an anniversary or birthday. We have all seen posts stating that someone is "in a relationship," but have you considered writing that on a post for the entire world to see?

Does your mate take a lunch to work? Napkins can be a great canvas for a little love note or drawing. And remember Dr. Dan's prescription from the previous chapter—texting is a great way to express a little (or big) flirt. Make a play list of love songs, and play it. And here's an oldie but goodie—Dan's parents were almost expelled from college back in the day for playing footsies under the table at mealtime. Gasp! Fun flirts set the stage for more flirting, giving invitation for kicking it up a notch.

Caress: The next level of romancing, your mate uses the caress to communicate love and the desire for deeper intimacy. This is touching, stroking, fondling, petting—a gentle expression of sexual passion inviting a sensual response. Through caressing you say to your partner, "I enjoy touching and being touched by you. My love for you is deep and pleasant. It is my desire to bring you great pleasure." Some caressing can be carefully enjoyed in public view. As it progresses, though, wise discretion is advised.

To entice or awaken is one side of the coin, but the other side is to be truly available. If you caress your mate sensuously in the morning, then are untouchable the rest of the day, your lover could be left feeling confused and frustrated. Don't make it a habit to leave your partner dangling. Ask God to help you perceive when it is time to progress on to the next level.

Arouse: As sexual anticipation grows, it becomes easy to admit that you are truly excited and want to share intense pleasure together. You shift into a new, sensational gear. Subtle arousal can be secretly enjoyed in public places. Blatant seduction, however, must always be done in private. There is no denying it now. It's time to play!

God gave both women and men five senses that *all* have roles in the awesome experience of sexual arousal:

- Enticing words are *heard.*
- Seductive postures are *seen.*
- Darting tongues *taste.*
- Body scents are *smelled.*
- Hands *touch* erogenous zones.

For maximal gratification from arousal, it is important to engage *all* your senses. Allow your partner to see and enjoy the sensual body God gave *you.* Of course, there are also times when arousal can be accelerated by closing eyes.

*Experiencing one another's bodies in
a boldly sexual setting can be extremely exciting
for both husbands and wives.*

With increasing arousal you will be well prepared to enter the highest level of sexual enticement.

Consummate: Yet another verb, *consummate* means to make marriage *complete* by having sex. It is the culminating act bringing perfection to this covenant of marriage. This is why, after God brought Adam and Eve together, the Bible states, "For this reason a man will leave his father and mother and be united to his wife, and they will become one flesh. The man and his wife were both naked, and they felt no shame" (Genesis 2:24–25).

Two lovers. Naked. Unashamed. One flesh. This truly is supernatural. It is divine. Both husband and wife are compelled by love to be intimate. And they are free to enjoy sexual stimulation—often culminating in penile/vaginal intercourse—with orgasm for both partners. Ooh la la—feeling fabulous!

Every level of enticement can be satisfying and should frequently be enjoyed. But there is something special about a man and woman privately experiencing the ultimate intimacy of sexual union. It was not good for the man to be alone. So God made him a helper, a companion. And that was said to be *very good* (Genesis 2:18; 1:31).

The Beauty of Seduction

Julie's marriage seemed to have become stale. Eat. Sleep. Work. Too much work, in fact. Her husband, John, had been ridiculously busy at the office. Each evening when he got home, he was kind but not energetic.

One evening their teens were at a youth meeting (hallelujah for good youth programs at church!) when John was expected to arrive home. Julie knew this was a wise time to awaken her husband to love.

Beginning at the door from the garage, she left a trail of her clothing as she undressed. The trail led from the garage through the bedroom to the bath where she sat waiting in the tub filled with bubbles. Candles were outlining the tub. There were two glasses of wine, cheese and crackers, and grapes to feed each other. John was thrilled to rediscover how enticing his wife could be. May it suffice to say that John was quickly rejuvenated within minutes after getting home?

Yes, *a lady can and should seduce her husband.* And it is proper for a gentleman to seduce his wife too. Romantic allurement is a great complement to the one being enticed, regardless of who makes the first move. Seduction expresses the desire to experience the pleasures of life together as a couple. It is a way of restating the commitment that "you are the one for me." Also, receptivity to sexual advances says, "I will freely share my body with you to satisfy your needs."

To be at its best, sexual enticement must be done with great patience, gentleness, and self-control.

These are fruit *of* the Spirit (Galatians 5:22–23) that can only be received *by* the Spirit. Ask God to fill you with His Spirit so that His fruit will be evident in the way you love your mate. The most satisfying kind of romance grows from the sharing of true *agape* love.

Knock, and the door will be opened for God's perfect love to flood your marriage relationship. His love brings the purest form of intimacy possible between husband and wife.

Sex Is Good!

Many who have grown up in church develop a bias against the nobility and decency of sex. We were taught during adolescence that sexual relations were dangerous and should be avoided at all costs. Sex was sin. Needless to say, it can be difficult after marriage to suddenly enjoy something that was clearly sinful during the time of courtship.

God created the heavens and the earth exactly as He desired them to be. Remember that on the sixth day, after humans were created male and female, God saw that "it was very good" (Genesis 1:31). After the fall in the garden of Eden, Adam and Eve suddenly became aware of their nakedness—they began questioning the goodness of the wonderful gift of sexuality they had received from God. Yet the goodness of the gift had not changed.

We live in the kingdom of light. God is fully pleased when we romance, seduce, and sexually enjoy one another within the safe playground of marriage. His supernatural love flowing between husband and wife brings the ultimate pleasures of sexual satisfaction. We were born to love.

If memories of sexual sin are holding you back from fully enjoying intimacy in marriage, don't look back. Forgive. Repent. Ask the Holy Spirit to renew your mind and heal your memories. Like the apostle Paul before you, there is one thing you need to do: "Forgetting what is behind and straining toward what is ahead, press on toward the goal that is before you" (Philippians 3:13–14). And you also need to remember, "There is now no condemnation for those who are in Christ Jesus" (Romans 8:1). God desires you to be free to enjoy every aspect of holy matrimony—including sexual intimacy. Our Father wants you and your mate to celebrate your glorious freedom together through the pleasure of superb sex!

What does God have to say about sexual satisfaction in marriage? We love what is written about this in the *Spirit Filled Life Bible*, which is edited by Jack Hayford: "By the mere inclusion of the Song of Solomon in the Bible, God makes a strong statement that sexual intimacy is not a lower or a base instinct to be suppressed or overcome. Rather, His intention is for sexual intimacy within marriage to be fulfilling, passionate and exciting."[3]

And the writer of Proverbs says:

As a loving deer and a graceful doe,
Let her breasts satisfy you at all times;

---

3   *Spirit Filled Life Bible: A Personal Study Bible Unveiling All God's Fullness in All God's Word (New King James Version)*, Jack Hayford, Ed., (Nashville: Thomas Nelson, 2002), 869.

And always be enraptured with her love
(Proverbs 5:19, NKJV).

Both you and your partner need sexual encounter. This can be done in a routine and perfunctory manner, or it can follow the lead of God's written Word to be romantic and sensual. Sex can be seen as an obligation or be appreciated as the wonderful opportunity that it is. There is a more excellent way.

Romancing your mate is a joyful adventure. Enticing your lover toward physical intimacy brings blessings to both of you. Entice boldly, entice often, and entice well. Each effort of enticement is valuable in the fine art of lovemaking.

DR. DAN'S PRESCRIPTIONS FOR ENTICE

* Use mouthwash in front of your partner as a tip you will soon need a kiss.
* Agree to flirt all day, but not finish until a predetermined time.
* Lie on a couch with your heads on opposite ends. Use hands to…
* How many "E's" (erections) can hubby have over one weekend? Make sure he remembers the last one.

5

Explore

We love honeymoon stories. Patty and Robert were both virgins when they got married. They had agreed to use natural family planning as a means of birth control. Here they were, at a gorgeous beach resort, hungry for each other after months of waiting. And wouldn't you know it— Patty was ovulating on their honeymoon.

These two were determined to have fun in spite of not being able to consummate their marriage for a few days. Patty and Robert took great delight in exploring each other's bodies. They could freely touch each other and see each other. They were having a great time pleasuring each other without intercourse. Later, when it was "safe" to play, they told us they were much more relaxed and comfortable together than they ever could have been on their wedding night. As I (Dan) like to say, "Delayed gratification is still gratification."

What a wonderful way for a couple to learn how to give and receive pleasure. Sexual play begins with wife and husband exploring one another's bodies—discovering together what satisfies each of them. Sexually successful spouses continue to learn new lovemaking skills through the years.

Lovemaking should never become dull or routine. The value of an exploratory play-plan never goes away.

God established this law for Israel: "If a man has recently married, he must not be sent to war or have any other duty laid on him. For one year he is to be free to stay at home and *bring happiness to the wife* he has married" (Deuteronomy 24:5). This is a joyful work assignment from our wise and loving Father!

How does a man use sex in bringing happiness to the wife he has married? And, while we are at it, what are the best ways a woman can sexually arouse and please her husband? Let's briefly explore intimate touch to uncover clues that will enhance your sexual enjoyment.

Erogenous Zones

Skin is by far the largest organ of the body. Our surface layer is twenty-two square feet in size and weighs eight pounds.[1] At different depths within the skin are buried numerous types of specialized receptors that are constantly available for stimulation. Each sends its particular message to the brain where it is analyzed and interpreted as touch, pressure, temperature, vibration, or pain.

We are keenly aware of these sensations that provide us with information, protection, and the ability to accomplish

---

1 "Skin," *National Geographic*: http://science.nationalgeographic.com/science/health-and-human-body/human-body/skin-article (accessed 9/10/2014).

tasks. Perhaps the most pleasant of those tasks is lovemaking in marriage.

Each category of sensory receptor in the skin plays its own unique role in sexual encounter. Every square inch of skin surface can make a sensational contribution toward enjoying sex-play, but there are certain regions of the body that are particularly sensitive to stimulation. Skillfully touching them increases sexual appetite and leads to heightened levels of sexual arousal. These **erogenic** areas are commonly referred to as **erogenous zones**.

Although men are a bit more focused on the desire for direct genital stimulation, the locations of erogenous zones for both husbands and wives are quite similar. There is much variation from one person to another as to which areas have the most **erotic** potential. Because of this, we recommend trying them all!

Hands are very sensitive and expressive because the density of skin receptors is extremely high, especially in the fingertips. Holding hands is relaxing and soothing for almost all lovers. Your fingers can signal sexual desire by stroking and squeezing any erogenic area of your partner in sensual ways. Tactile enticement brings pleasure and arousal to you and your mate.

A gentle *foot* massage can bring satisfying relief from the stresses of a long day. This kind of sensuous caressing is calming at least, and for some it can lead to dramatic sexual excitement. It is possible that this is a crossover response since sensations from the feet and genitals are processed adjacent to each other in the middle fissure of the brain. A bottle of nice massage lotion might be a more exciting gift than you have realized!

The thin skin on the inner side of the *arms* and *legs* can be quite erotic as well. Gentle circular motions just above the kneecaps are arousing for some if you press firmly enough to avoid tickling. So when was the last time you told your lover you like his or her knees? Stroking movements along your partner's inner thighs may raise the level of sexual excitement rapidly, particularly when done very high—near the **perineum** and gluteal fold.

Exploring is really fun, right?

There are also several areas on the *head* that can be used to produce delightfully sensuous feelings during lovemaking. Mouth-to-mouth kissing. *Lips. Tongues.* Delicious! Increasing the frequency and depth of tongue penetration communicates passionate desire to most lovers. Massaging the *face* and squeezing and kissing behind the *earlobes* are also sensuous ways to entice your mate. Stimulating the *scalp* by rubbing may be quite erogenic also. Firmly but painlessly pulling a handful of hair will push some wives and husbands from **high plateau** on through orgasmic release. We playfully refer to **orgasm** or **climax** as the big "O."

The *breasts* are strongly erogenous in most women as well as in many men. Some can enjoy climaxing through breast stimulation alone. Nipples contain a high density of specialized nerve endings, smooth muscle, and erectile tissue. The surrounding pink areola is also quite sensitive to touch due to the presence of many small hairs. The pressure used in the touching of breasts and squeezing of nipples must be varied depending on the happy recipient's level of arousal. Speaking the words "harder" or "softer" to your spouse will optimize this pleasurable experience.

As touching and rubbing descends from the collarbone and underarm to the sides of the ribs and *abdomen*, the erogenous zones become more effective in sexual arousal. The farther south of the *navel* you stimulate your partner, the more rapidly desire will grow. Make use of this "happy trail" regularly.

Gentle stroking and caressing of skin can produce feelings of well-being and peace quite apart from sexual arousal. A four-footed pet demonstrates this kind of response during a tummy rub by its owner. Love can be well communicated to your spouse by gently touching in a pleasurable but nondemanding way. Touch is a language of love whether or not sex is desired at the moment.

For most people, the *pelvis* is the most erogenous of all body regions. The **genitals, perianal** area, and perineum (region between the two) make up a majority of the sacral S2–S5 sensory input to the brain that is critical in arousal and orgasm. Wives and husbands who desire sexual encounter find it pleasurable and exciting when these areas are caressed. However, most will require direct genital stimulation if an "O" is desired.

Many men can be brought to climax by vigorous genital massage alone. Ladies, you have a sweet choice to make: which of your body parts would you like to use in this genital massage of your man? In women it is more common that foreplay is required to set the stage for enjoying the higher levels of arousal. Men, if you want your woman to squeal in ecstasy, you will need to delay pulling your trigger until she is very high.

> *All of us will find sex to be more gratifying*
> *when we know how to sensuously make use of all*
> *the erogenous zones God designed for us to enjoy.*

Let's read what He inspired a wise king to write about the sensuous enjoyment of making love:

> Your stature is like that of the palm,
> and your breasts like clusters of fruit.
> I said, "I will climb the palm tree;
> I will take hold of its fruit."
> May your breasts be like the clusters of the vine,
> the fragrance of your breath like apples,
> and your mouth like the best wine
> (Song of Solomon 7:7–9).

Touching a particular area of the body may be arousing

for one person and annoying for another. Therefore, there is great variation among individuals as to which erogenic areas are the most pleasurable. Communicate clearly to your mate which areas increase or decrease your level of enjoyment. Experiment. Explore. If at first you don't succeed, then try, try, and try again.

God Made Man, and He Said He Was Very Good

For many years, Dr. Dan worked in a large, multi-specialty medical clinic with well over a hundred doctors. One year a "Hairy Leg Contest" was held as a fundraiser for the United Way. A bulletin board was set up with photographs of all the male physicians' bare legs from the knees down. Employees were to try to match the legs with the doctor.

One of Dan's nurses took me (Linda) to see the display. Right away I was able to find Dan's legs. The nurse was shocked that I could recognize them so quickly and easily. My point is this: I want to know Dan and *all* of his parts. I want to see and recognize him from every angle.

The better we know each other,
the more intimate we can become. Exploration is fun.

You will also want to know every part of your mate's body. To help in your exploration we will walk you through basic sexual anatomy. (See the glossary at the back of this book for male and female internal and external anatomy graphics.)

A man's **penis** is an interesting and amazing appendage

created by God to bring great pleasure to both husband and wife. For simplicity, let's talk about the penis in its *erect*, steely state that occurs early in sexual arousal. By the way, steely *erections*, big "E's," come in handy when you want "I" (intercourse). We think Old MacDonald and his wife had a lot of fun on his E-I-E-I-O farm.

The rounded end of the penis is called the **glans penis**—a very sensitive area due to its thin surface and the presence of many wonderful nerve endings. The glans is prominently seen in circumcised men, but is somewhat hidden by the hood of the *foreskin* in those who have not had this operation. The small opening at the tip is the *urethra* or urine tube. Wives are often relieved to learn that it is nearly impossible for urine to come through this tube during erection or orgasm. God designed the penis to emit more urgently needed liquids during sexual play, such as **semen** containing **sperm** for fertilization.

The tissue between the glans and the pubic area is the *shaft* of the penis, which is wrapped by very thin skin. The top of the shaft, facing forward when erect is the **frenulum** of the penis, which is often the most sexually arousing point of a man's anatomy. Wives, did you get that? Your hubby will be very happy for you to be friendly with his frenulum.

Within the penile shaft there are three columnar structures that periodically fill with blood, causing "E's." One is a *spongy tissue* that wraps around the urine tube inside the penis and connects to the very similar glans on the outside. The other two cylinders fill the remainder of the shaft. These *cavernous structures* also engorge with blood during arousal. Because the connective tissue around the penis has a limited capacity to stretch, the enlarging of these three causes the penis to become very stiff and hard. Seeing and feeling the husband's erect penis often increases the wife's sexual arousal. Erection also makes it much easier for entering her vagina during **intercourse**, which is also known as **coitus** or **copulation**.

> *For most men the frenulum plays*
> *a major role in their sexual stimulation.*

When a husband holds his wife in a standing embrace, her body pushes against his frenulum. The same area is stimulated when one of them moves while lying on top of the other. In the high plateau of arousal during intercourse, the glans and frenulum of the husband push against the firm cervix of the wife, bringing wonderful pleasure to both.

God shows His wisdom and amazing love to couples by designing the penis in just this way. With each deep thrust against the cervix, the man's arousal increases until climax is achieved. Semen pours over and pushes through the cervical opening, giving the very best odds of fertilization. In Genesis 1:28, we read that God told Adam and Eve to "be fruitful and increase in number." Our Creator made it sheer pleasure for both of them, and also for us, to follow His command.

Beneath the penis are the two **testicles** (testes) that are housed within the thin, loose skin of the **scrotum** (scrotal sac). This skin shrinks and expands intermittently, keeping the testes slightly cooler than normal body temperature, maximizing the fertilization potential of the *sperm* they produce. In cooler temperatures this shrinkage of the scrotum can become uncomfortable for the husband during sex-play, resulting in a need to add body contact or to cover the area with a blanket to relieve the pain. Erection and sexual enjoyment can end quickly when any type of pain occurs.[2]

God created a complex design for producing Adam's semen. Sperm produced in the testes is stored in the **epididymis** and then transferred into the pelvis via the **vas deferens.** The sperm is combined with fluids from the **seminal vesicles** (70 percent of volume) and the **prostate gland** (30 percent of volume) to form fluid that is deposited into the beginning of the urethra.[3] This happy triad is called semen. Once this has occurred, an "O" is eminent and the "point of no return" for **ejaculation** has been passed. Going over the top is generally a sweet time for both husband and wife. And you, manly men, make sure your wives are satisfied before you get all sleepy.

God Made Woman, and Didn't He Do an Amazing Job?

Female breast development begins in early puberty as a response to increasing levels of **estrogen** and **progesterone**.

---

2 As an aside, if you are trying to make a baby, you might want to avoid hot tubs for a while because heat decreases fertility.

3 For further information, see Robert L. Crooks, *Our Sexuality* (2005). Note in particular chapter 5, "Male Sexual Anatomy and Physiology."

Several kinds of glandular breast tissues grow at this time that are distinctly different from what is found in a man. Fatty tissue increases in the breast, and the ***areola*** surrounding the nipple flattens and enlarges in diameter. By the way, a woman's breasts are rarely symmetrical. Also, nipple size and characteristics vary greatly from one woman to another.

Sexual stimulation can cause ***Montgomery's glands*** of the areola to secrete an oily lubricant; contraction of muscles makes hairs on the areola more prominent and leads to firm erection of the spongy nipple tissue. Wasn't it generous of God to allow both genders to have erections? A woman's perception of pleasure from pressure on her nipples (squeezing or gently biting) varies dramatically with the days of the menstrual cycle. Sexual arousal typically increases her desire for firmer pressure to be applied. Go for it, men. She will tell you when it is too much.

Women's sexual anatomy was brilliantly designed. The visible parts of a wife's genitals are a beautiful collection of amazing sexual tissues called the ***vulva***. Included in this grouping are the mons pubis, labia majora, labia minora, clitoris, and vaginal opening.

Starting from the top we find the ***mons pubis***—the skin and fatty padding under the skin that protects the pubic bone from the husband's pubic bone during intercourse. Most of a woman's pubic hair is found in this area. Extending downward left and right from the mons are the ***labia majora*** (outer lips) that come together again as they meet at the perineum just one inch in front of the rectum. Between the outer lips are two flaps of soft skin called the ***labia minora*** (inner lips). Out of view, beneath each of these hairless lips, is the corpus cavernosum of the ***clitoris***, a sponge-like structure that is three to five inches in length and becomes erect when filled by blood during arousal.[4] Yet another erection!

The ***glans clitoris*** (C-spot, sweet spot) is found where inner lips meet, just above the urethral opening. The clitoral hood, which is similar to the male foreskin, covers it. When the clitoris becomes erect with sexual arousal, the C-spot may protrude beyond the hood making it more visible and available for direct stimulation.

> *As far as scientists have been able to determine, the only known function of the clitoris is to provide sexual pleasure.*

The C-spot has more nerve endings than any other point on the skin of either man or woman. It was God's great pleasure to create woman in such a way that she could fully enjoy having sex with her man! Obviously there is a need for all married people to be ***cliterate***—to understand, utilize, and enjoy the clitoris. Men, explore this sweet spot if you want to put a sparkle in your lady's eyes.

Between the minor lips, a little below the urethral opening,

---

4 A. Giraldi and A. Graziottin, "Anatomy and Physiology of Women's Sexual Function," H. Porst and J. Buvat, Eds., *ISSM (International Society of Sexual Medicine) Standard Committee Book, Standard Practice in Sexual Medicine, Blackwell* (UK: Oxford, 2006), 289–304.

is the entrance to the ***vagina.*** This soft tissue is lubricated during foreplay by the two pea-sized ***Bartholin's glands*** found on the left and right, inside of the vaginal opening. These secretions improve the pleasure of stimulation in this area and make entrance of the penis more comfortable.

Extending across part of the vaginal opening is the ***hymen.*** This thin tissue has been thought to be an indicator of a female's virginity, but actually is a poor indicator for two reasons. First, a virgin can have no evidence of this structure. And second, much of the hymen can remain in a sexually active woman. "Despite horror stories about the pain and bleeding that accompany first intercourse, most women experience only minor discomfort and minimal bleeding."[5]

The vagina reaches far beyond the visible vulva. Its four-inch length grows longer with arousal. This normally collapsed tube is quite elastic, easily stretching to accept the average 5.57-inch erect male penis during intercourse.[6] Muscles in the wall can contract, applying exquisite pressure sensations to the husband. Vaginal secretions provide delightful lubrication for both partners during sexual play.

---

5 Paul and Lori Byerly, "The Female Genitals," *The Marriage Bed: Sex and Intimacy for Married Christians:* http://site.themarriagebed.com/biology/her-plumbing (accessed 9/5/2014).

6 Debby Herbenick, PhD, MPH, Michael Reece, PhD, MPH, Vanessa Schick, PhD, and Stephanie A. Sanders, PhD, "Erect Penile Length and Circumference Dimensions of 1,661 Sexually Active Men in the United States," *The Journal of Sexual Medicine*, vol. 11, issue 1 (January 2014): 93–101, which can be found at http://onlinelibrary.wiley.com/doi/10.1111/jsm.12244/abstract, (accessed 12/19/2014).

Near the end of the vagina is a one-inch firm circular structure called the **cervix.** Its small opening, or **external os**, is the beginning of the *uterus*, a muscular organ with thick walls and a hollow space that is lined by the **endometrium.** Strong contractions occur in the uterus and vagina during sexual climax.

Deeper within a woman's body are the two **ovaries.** They lie in the pelvis on either side of the uterus. With **ovulation,** one or more eggs are released by the ovaries into the fallopian tube to be carried into the uterus for fertilization by sperm. Along with the adrenal glands, the ovaries secrete the hormone estrogen, which is responsible for the development of secondary sex characteristics in women and maintaining the functional state of the mature reproductive organs. Testosterone and progesterone are also produced within the ovaries.

If your head is swimming from all this anatomical talk, just hang on a little longer. The fun is about to begin.

Stimulation

We recommend much variety in sexual play, but a guide to the basics of really great sex can be helpful. Begin by touching, stroking, and caressing the arms, legs, and head, which are less erotic areas that are further from the core. Then progress to stimulation of the more sensitive erogenous zones of the breasts, abdomen, and genitals as foreplay advances. Pleasure your partner by gently rubbing and massaging their chest and abdominal area before heading south.

Open your *eyes* to enjoy seeing what you are caressing. And watch with awe as your lover gives you pleasure. Allow the one you love to see your body as well. This is playfully referred to as eye candy.

Enjoy the excitement of giving and receiving a lingering gaze. It is arousing to know you are looking and being looked at in intimate ways.

Fingers are wonderful tools for bringing pleasure to your partner. Lubrication with lotions and oils is helpful and fun. Touch the erogenous zones using a variety of movements, pressures, and speeds. Avoid tickling unless your lover enjoys it. *Hands* speak passion by pressing firmly and deeply, and then share excitement through clutching and grasping for more.

Pushing against your lover with *hips* can be extremely arousing, even when intercourse is not occurring at the time. *Legs* can be powerfully stimulating when pushed against buttocks, genitals, or the perineum. Through variation of position, pressure, and movement, the touching of bodies communicates clearly when a strong sexual message is desired.

Use your *lips* for light kissing of the mouth. Penetrate deeper with the *tongue* to awaken desire. It is important to use a variety of angles, lip pressures, and tongue movements as you give and receive pleasure. When your partner is receptive, move on to kissing ears, neck, nipples, and other areas that bring delight. If you and your mate are in agreement, **oral sex** can be a most powerful source of sexual excitement.

When a man arouses his wife by kissing her genitals (vulva), it is called **cunnilingus**. This form of foreplay is alluded to as the beloved speaks to her lover, "Let my lover come into his garden and taste its choice fruits" (Song of Solomon 4:16). Oral stimulation of a woman is particularly effective for stimulating the very sensitive C-spot and is often the easiest way to bring her to orgasm.

Fellatio is the scientific name used when a woman sexually stimulates her husband by kissing his penis or scrotum. In Scripture, the beloved refers to this version of oral sex by saying, "I delight to sit in his shade, and his fruit is sweet to my taste" (Song of Solomon 2:3). Only the wife should decide whether semen is released inside or outside of her mouth. Swallowing this less than a teaspoon of fluid containing sugar, salt, protein, and only one calorie[7] does not add risk to the oral sex encounter.

For both husband and wife, *any* sex outside the safe playground of marriage brings the risk of sexually transmitted disease into the union.

Many men find fellatio particularly enjoyable because it simulates the sensations experienced during vaginal intercourse. It is also convenient as it can be enjoyed when intercourse is not an option (e.g. in the late stage of pregnancy). Climax reached in this way is often perceived as more intense and satisfying

---

7 Derek H. Owen and David F. Katz, "A Review of the Physical and Chemical Properties of Human Semen and the Formulation of a Semen Simulant," *Journal of Andrology*, vol. 26, issue 4 (July–August 2005): 459–469.

than when it is achieved by digital massage (otherwise known as a hand job).[8] When oral sex is performed on either husband or wife, extreme cleanliness is advised to optimize the experience for both partners.

Another type of sexual stimulation that is sometimes controversial in Christian circles is ***masturbation***—self-stimulation of the genitals, usually for the purpose of enjoying an "O." As with other sensitive subjects concerning sexuality, couples should use discernment from the Holy Spirit when considering this option.

Masturbation in secret by either husband or wife can be detrimental to the relationship because of its self-centered focus. It can also lower ***libido***, temporarily leaving one partner with little interest in play at a time when the other is in need of sexual relations. Another problem is that private masturbation is frequently associated with lustful thoughts toward others outside the marriage or memories of pornographic images.

On the other hand, some couples use self-stimulation in very positive ways. During times of extended separation, spousal encouragement of masturbation can relieve uncomfortable sexual tension and bond lovers together from afar as they imagine being *with their covenantal partner*. Some married couples choose to do this during phone conversations or video chats.

Not always done alone, self-touch can also be used as a

---

8 "Acts and Pleasure—Men," which is a survey of 578 men. *The Marriage Bed: Sex and Intimacy for Married Christians:* http://site.themarriagebed.com/surveys/acts-and-pleasure-–-men (accessed 9/ 5/2014).

supplement to stimulation provided by the partner in shared lovemaking. In this setting masturbation can be a visual demonstration of what feels best, teaching a mate how to best provide the most pleasurable sensations.

Anal intercourse is a subject discussed and considered within many marriages. One in five women, ages twenty to forty, accept anal sex with their partner.[9] This is far from a new idea as artistic representations of heterosexual anal sex go back to AD 300.[10] Surprisingly, it is neither sanctioned nor excluded by Scripture. In fact, we have not found a verse in the Bible that refers to this practice at all. Couples wanting to avoid pregnancy have sometimes opted for anal sex.

Proponents of anal sex claim that it presents no risk to husband or wife when performed in the "right" way using adequate lubrication. But medical research has not been published supporting this view. Conversely, much scientific data points to the dangers associated with entrance of the penis into the rectum.

Among women who experience anal sex, 9 percent find it to be unbearably painful.[11] Stretching caused by an erect penis

---

9   "National Survey of Sexual Health and Behavior," which was a survey done by the School of Health, Physical Education, and Recreation at Indiana University, Bloomington: http://www.nationalsexstudy.indiana.edu (accessed 9/5/2014).

10 "Anal Sex—Sin, Bad Idea, or What?" *The Marriage Bed: Sex and Intimacy for Married Christians:* http://site.themarriagebed.com/sexuality/anal-sex (accessed 9/6/2014).

11 Aleksandar Štulhofer and Dea Ajdukovi, "Should We Take Anodyspareunia Seriously? A Descriptive Analysis of Pain During Receptive Anal Intercourse in Young Heterosexual Women," *Journal of Sex and Marital Therapy*, vol. 37, issue 5 (2011).

can also aggravate hemorrhoids, result in rectal fistulas, and cause anal tissue tears that lead to rectal prolapse.[12]

A British medical study showed a marked increase in fecal incontinence for homosexual men who received this form of intercourse.[13] Anal sex is also known to cause urinary tract infection (UTI) in men.[14] Sexual freedom is of great value in the marriages of believers, but we recommend avoiding this edgy option due to the clear medical risks involved.

Variety is the spice of life given to us by God to enjoy. You and your mate will be blessed when you use variety and creativity to enrich lovemaking.

Is something working well today as you touch and arouse one another? Stay with it for a while, but don't overdo even a good thing. No one enjoys being stuck in a rut! Move on to another location, position, or technique. You can always return to doing "that" once again to complete the pleasuring of your lover. True classics never go out of style.

And speaking of classics, traditional *intercourse*—penis into vagina—remains the most popular sexual activity. We

---

12 "Anal Sex—Sin, Bad Idea, or What?" *op. cit.*

13 A. J. Miles, T. G. Allen-Mersh, and C. Wastell, "Effect of Anoreceptive Intercourse on Anorectal Function," *Journal of The Royal Society of Medicine*, Mar. 1993; 86(3): 144–147. This journal can be accessed at the US National Library of Medicine: http://www.ncbi.nlm.nih.gov/pmc/articles/PMC1293903/.

14 "Bacterial Urinary Tract Infections," The Merck Manual Professional Edition, last revision November 2013 by Talha H. Imam, MD, http://www.merckmanuals.com/professional/genitourinary_disorders/urinary_tract_infections_uti/bacterial_urinary_tract_infections.html (accessed 3/6/2015).

recommend maintaining this conventional approach while adding other techniques to your repertoire.

In our opinion, traditional "I" fosters the sense of the biblical one flesh, enhancing intimacy between husband and wife. The Greek word *proskollēthēsetai,*[15] which is translated as being "united" in Ephesians 5:31, means that husband and wife are sexually glued together in a face-to-face or eye-to-eye posture. Could this be why missionaries of old recommended this traditional position for play?

Men are more likely to climax when sex includes vaginal intercourse. On the other hand, women are more likely to orgasm when they engage in a variety of sex acts with or without vaginal intercourse.[16] Why not incorporate multiple techniques in your next lovemaking session? Enjoy learning the patterns that are best suited for bringing pleasure to both you and your mate.

Male or female, young or old, every lover has his or her favorite ways to be caressed and aroused during lovemaking. Our erogenous patterns of desire are as unique as fingerprints. Identify them. Know them. Use them. And don't forget to enjoy them!

---

15 *Strong's Exhaustive Concordance*, s.v. "*proskollēthēsetai*," Greek 4347.

16 "National Survey of Sexual Health and Behavior," which was a survey done by the School of Health, Physical Education, and Recreation at Indiana University, Bloomington: http://www.nationalsexstudy.indiana.edu (accessed 9/5/2014).

Arousal

Do you want to know what makes your heart go pitter-patter? It all begins with desire. Desire is birthed in the mind as an interest in sexual encounter, opening the door for *sexual arousal* to occur. In both men and women, **epinephrine** (adrenaline) is released by the adrenal gland—raising the rate of the pulse, increasing depth of breathing, and elevating blood pressure. In arousal, the blood vessels in muscles dilate, increasing strength and physical capacity for lovemaking. Dilation of vessels within the skin of male and female genitals increases the redness and the deepness of their color. Nipples become firmer and darker in both sexes.

Early in a wife's arousal, her C-spot and the clitoral tissues beneath the labia minora fill with blood and become erect. Bartholin's glands release clear lubricant at the opening of the vagina, and the vaginal walls secrete milky liquid in preparation for receiving her husband's penis.

With even the thought of making love, the husband's penis fills with blood, causing it to enlarge. Sexual touch, however, is required to maintain his erection. As arousal advances, a small amount of thick, clear, salty fluid from the Cowper's glands (called *pre-ejaculate*) will appear at the urethral opening. This is not semen.

As sex-play continues, the level of excitement continues to rise, often more slowly for the woman than the man. *Plateau* is the very highest level of sexual arousal. Further increases occur in blood pressure, heart rate, and respiration. The uterus may shift its position, changing the angle of contact between his penis and her cervix. She might enjoy stronger stimulation of the clitoris now as her clitoral glans retracts behind its hood. His prostate fills quickly with milky fluid as he prepares for ejaculation. Both wife and husband feel the sensations of impending orgasm.

Orgasm

Orgasm (climax) is the sudden and dramatic release of sexual tension. This full-body response includes muscular contractions in the pelvis, cardiovascular changes, hormonal release, and sensations of intense pleasure. Both husbands and wives receive great joy in helping their partner hit the high note.

Men have a series of rhythmic contractions of the penis, perineum, and anus. The semen that has collected at the base of the urethra squirts out through its opening in powerful pulsations. This is called *ejaculation*.

Women have a similar series of spasms of the vagina, uterus, perineum, and anus. These contractions can force mucous out from the vagina along with secretions by **Skene's glands** exiting from two openings adjacent to the urethra. The expelling of these liquids is sometimes referred to as **female ejaculation**.

Some researchers refer to Skene's glands as the **female prostate gland**. Its degree of development is highly variable from woman to woman, being prominent in some and virtually absent in others. Because of this, the volume of secretions by the glands is also quite varied. Most women do not have visible ejaculation with orgasm. But in some the release of liquid can be very obvious. It is reassuring for both husband and wife to know that this expelled fluid is *not* urine; all degrees of female ejaculation, from none to a lot, are within the range of normal.

Interestingly, Skene's glands are thought to be the anatomical explanation for the *"G-spot"* described by the German gynecologist Ernst Grafenberg, both being located within the front wall of the vagina. As with massage of the male prostate, stimulation of the G-spot can produce pleasurable sensations that are sexually arousing. Only a minority of women has this bonus erogenic location.

Women who are successful at locating their G-spot may find it to be a wonderful asset to sex-play.

Orgasmic women are fairly equally divided into three groups. Only about one-third of these ladies are able to reach an "O" with intercourse. Another third can experience an "O" with intercourse accompanied by additional manual or oral stimulation. And, as you might expect, the remaining third only get to the happy high by techniques other than intercourse.[17]

For both men and women, while these wonderfully

---

17 "Female Orgasms: Myths and Facts," The Society of Obstetricians and Gynaecologists of Canada: http://sogc.org/publications/female-orgasms-myths-and-facts/ (accessed 11/1/2014).

pleasant pulsations are being enjoyed, heart rate, blood pressure, and breathing are reaching their peaks. The rate of phenylethylamine production in the brain increases during arousal and also peaks during orgasm. This causes ***dopamine*** to be released, resulting in the feeling of bliss. Sex raises testosterone levels in both men and women, increasing future capacity for arousal and providing a sense of virility. The concentration of ***serotonin*** in the brain also rises with orgasm. This natural antidepressant makes you feel cheerful, hopeful, and content. ***Oxytocin*** levels increase in the blood serum for both men and women at orgasm, inducing a sense of calmness and security that improves bonding between mates.[18]

The sensations experienced during sexual climax are remarkably variable. Orgasms in women feel different—clitoral or vaginal—depending upon what is being stimulated. Occasionally women do not feel the sensations of the pelvic floor spasms but still obtain the wonderful feelings of tranquility after reaching orgasm. Men also report quite varied orgasmic sensations depending on which part of their penis has been massaged. Body positions such as sitting, standing, and lying down have major impact on the quality and intensity of pleasure received. Most of us have our favorite position for going over the top. Do you know your mate's?

---

18 Carmichael MS, Warburton VL, Dixen J, Davidson JM, "Relationships among Cardiovascular, Muscular, and Oxytocin Responses during Human Sexual Activity," *Archives of Sexual Behavior*, Feb. 1994, 23(1): 59–79.

Timing also plays a significant role in sexual response. God is wise when He tells wives and husbands to "not deprive each other except by mutual consent and for a time…. Then come together again" (1 Corinthians 7:5). Orgasms occurring after a long period of abstinence may be less intense than those enjoyed during more regular sex-play. Arousal within a day of a previous climax might be more challenging, but can produce an "O" of amazing intensity. The strength of any climax is enhanced when high plateau is reached more than once before heading on over the summit (E-I-E-I-O). No matter what kind of "O" occurs, it will leave you in a contented, happy place.

What is going on during that peaceful, easy feeling after orgasm? Most lovers are very relaxed at this point due to the burst of **endorphins** (short for "endogenous morphine") binding the morphine receptors in their brains. Men often quickly fall to sleep—a true complement given to their wives for excellence in lovemaking. Blood swiftly escapes from nipples and genitalia, relieving the engorgement that is uncomfortable if orgasmic relief does not occur. Erections rapidly resolve, and interest in sex is often gone for a time.

After climaxing, nearly all men enter a **refractory period** of minutes to days, averaging about half an hour.[19] With rare exceptions it is impossible for them to maintain an erection or have additional orgasms during this phase. Although multiple

19 Bernice Kanner, *Are You Normal About Sex, Love, and Relationships?* (New York: St. Martin's Griffin, 2003), 52.

climaxes are possible for women, many enter a similar period of time when it is unlikely that they can be aroused.

Back to Eden

When it comes to giving and receiving intense sexual pleasure, all of us would like our marriage partners to call us the wizard of a-h-h-h-h-h-s.

It is great to know the details of sexual anatomy. We are wise to learn effective techniques for arousal. There is value in understanding what is happening when we find ourselves in the grip of sexual passion. But there is more.

In the wilderness near Canaan, God gave Moses the plans for the tabernacle where His presence would dwell. How could any man accomplish such a beautiful and magnificent plan? God sent Bezalel to Moses from the tribe of Judah and "filled him with the Spirit of God, with skill, ability and knowledge" (Exodus 35:30–31). He received all that was needed to lead a troop of "skilled craftsmen" (Exodus 26–39) who perfectly followed God's design for constructing the tabernacle.

As was Bezalel, those who follow Christ are filled with the Holy Spirit. He prepares each husband and wife to be fully skilled in the craft of making love. Through God's Spirit leading, teaching, and inspiring you to love, you can receive all that is required to enjoy the astonishing sex life that God has designed and that you've always desired.

God has blessed you with gifts of anatomy and physiology—body responses that are pleasurable beyond description—so that you and your lover would truly enjoy intimacy.

> *Through the Spirit, you've been given skill, ability, and knowledge of how to give and receive love beyond your imagination.*

His plan for your magnificent marriage began "in the beginning" in a romantic garden called *Eden*.

The word *Eden* in Hebrew means "delight" or "enjoyment."[20] Eden was a garden filled with pleasure. Adam and Eve were given hearts to love and bodies that could sensuously come together, becoming physically and spiritually one flesh in marriage. When you seduce your spouse just for fun, it is a form of recreation. In a sense you are re-creating the ambiance of Eden within y*our* marriage. You were created to explore and enjoy sexual play.

We counsel with many serious adults—so serious and wounded that they truly cannot fathom how to explore and play—who cannot give themselves permission to experience pleasure. If you are one of these dear ones, we encourage you to rediscover lighthearted, nonsexual play. Escape to a playground to swing and go down slides. Eat an ice cream cone.

---

20 "The name Eden in the Bible," *Abarim Publications*: http://www.abarim-publications.com/Meaning/Eden.html#.VPsT-VPF8l4 (accessed 3/7/2015).

Learning how to play, laugh, and enjoy yourself is a giant step toward being able to receive pleasure in lovemaking.

Keep your heart and your mind wide open. Embrace liberty. Explore. Simply and sensually play.

DR. DAN'S PRESCRIPTIONS FOR EXPLORE

* Agree to excite each other as much as possible—no hands or intercourse allowed.
* Play "E-I-E-I-O." Old MacDonald sure knew how to have fun. How many "O's" in a day, during a week, or while on vacation can you possibly have?
* Light a number of candles (so you have adequate light but with a romantic atmosphere) and explore the body parts we discussed in this chapter, especially the ones you are not as familiar with (remember the perineum and the frenulum).

6

Imagine

Children are playfully imaginative. Our oldest son has always loved music. When he was a toddler, we would often find him holding a hairbrush as a microphone singing his little heart out. To this day every time we hear the simple praise song "I Love You, Lord," we immediately envision our son with the hairbrush lifting up his voice to the Lord.

Our granddaughter loved being a mermaid when she was little. She would lie on the floor as if she was a beautiful mermaid swimming in the sea. And what young boy does not want to be a superhero or sport's star? It is common for us to encourage children to use their vivid and playful imaginations. Why not do the same with our spouses?

Albert Einstein once said that your imagination can take you everywhere.[1] A good imagination is great for sex! It is creative and it is fun. And, yes, it can be sanctified.

> With a sanctified—holy and pure—imagination, we can become even better lovers with our spouses.

---

1 Alice Calaprice, *The Ultimate Quotable Einstein*, (Princeton: Princeton University Press and The Hebrew University of Jerusalem, 2011), 481.

Allow yourself to daydream about being an astounding lover. Yes, you! Your lovemaking can be amazing, hot, romantic, and playful. What would this look like?

Why not try a little imaginative exercise right now? Imagine yourself being sexually *playful* with your mate. How would the scene look different if you were aiming for *romantic* foreplay? Next, visualize *steamy hot* sex with your lover. Different scenarios present fun variety and bring entertaining experiences to your sex life.

Steve and Susan decided to take our advice one day as they were frolicking in the bedroom. Steve had Susan sit on his lap face-to-face while he sat on the top of a barstool. Penetration was too deep for Susan's comfort, so the experiment did not last long. They completed their play that day in a less unusual way.

A few weeks later while traveling together, Susan ordered strawberry shortcake to be brought up to their room in a nice hotel. When Steve came out of the bathroom in his bathrobe, he was happy to find whipped cream placed on Susan in two prominent locations. Her imagination led them to a more delicious result than the previous barstool fantasy. We bet they both had a twinkle in their eyes after their afternoon delight.

Sometimes what we have fantasized plays out beautifully in our lovemaking. Oh, yeah. But sometimes the fantasy is much more pleasant than the reality. We end up laughing and saying, "At least we tried." It is good to be able to laugh together about sexual blunders. We have all had a few of these. Don't be afraid to try out sexual fantasies. But always be willing to leave them behind if your mate does not want to go along with your dream or it didn't work out the way you expected. The feelings of your lover always trump what might seem to be fun in the imaginings of your mind.

Since the Holy Spirit is our teacher and guide, have you considered asking Him to teach you how to be a better lover? A more creative player? He loves to be welcomed into your lovemaking—the most intimate of playgrounds.

Creative Play

In our chapter about exploring, we provided you with some great information about your bodies and how they respond sexually. The anatomy and physiology are easily seen, felt, and measured. But the most vital functions of sexual encounter lie beyond the limitations of our human perception, truly beyond our ability to understand.

The most powerful erogenous zone of all exists within the invisible, immeasurable boundaries of the mind. At its epicenter is the imagination.

The endless variety seen in plants, animals, and people on the earth show the limitless creativity of our Creator, God. And remember that we are made in His image. That means *you* are creative! God's desire is that we would delightfully use our imaginations to thoroughly enjoy the amazing gift of sex. Can you imagine stepping into a higher level of lovemaking?

This would bring great pleasure to you and your mate—and to your Father in heaven as well. Imagination is the key to stepping it up a notch as a lover.

Be creative in expressing romantic thoughts to your partner before, during, and after sexual play. Surprise the one you love with words, actions, gestures, and gifts that express the passion of your affection. Touching, caressing, stimulating, pleasuring, making, and receiving advances—all of these can be done in new and creative ways even after decades of marriage. There are no limitations to the capacity of our imaginations or the astounding creativity God joyfully shares with His children. We do not want ho-hum sex! Lovemaking should *never* be dull or routine.

A sweet couple told us their delightful honeymoon story a few years ago. Julie and Phil spent the first few days of their marriage at a nice hotel in San Francisco. One evening they decided to have a little fun in the shower together. They were having a good ol' time rubbing soap all over each other's bodies, which led to sex while standing up in the shower. After toweling off and returning to the bedroom, they were surprised to find the maid had been in the room, turning back their bed. Blushing and laughing, they were sure she had heard the gleeful sounds coming from the shower. We bet they remembered to display the "do not disturb" sign on the door the next time.

Few couples will find intercourse while standing up to be their favorite method of play. Yet many want to try this creative adventure at least once. Why not consider it? Whether or not you enjoy the position (or are even physically able to complete the act), it will be an encounter worth remembering.

Our Father wants you to use creativity received from heaven for things that are important, like good sex! He will guide your imagination to come up with what is best for you and your mate. Imagination can lead to many creative variations in how to play. May we offer a few suggestions to help you get started?

It's amazing how different caressing and touching feels with you and your partner in uncommon body positions. An easy one to try is with the woman's head in the normal sleeping position and the man's head near her feet. This change in perspective stimulates creativity in touching, caressing, and pleasuring. When is the last time you kissed your mate's toes?

Another sensuous position is for the wife to lie on her tummy across the foot of the bed while her husband stands on the floor beside her, massaging her entire body with warm lotion. Next, reverse roles. Then try this with your partner lying on his or her back instead of the tummy.

One day you might enjoy snuggling with both of you completely under a sheet on the bed, as if you were playing in a tent. See your partner in a whole new light as it filters through the cloth. You might be surprised how enjoyable sex will be in this novel location created in the middle of your same ol' bedroom.

Music. Candles. Incense. All of these add sensual variety that increases excitement and pleasure.

Install a rheostat (dimmer) for the light fixture to vary the illumination of the room. We are sure you will like the soft light now and then. And even satin sheets feel cool and smooth against lovers' skin. But be careful to not fall out of bed—satin sheets are slippery! Although sometimes falling out of bed is the perfect thing to do.

When you desire more variety in lovemaking, use your God-given creativity to play in different and innovative locations. Make it your goal to have sex in every room of the house. Well, perhaps not every room. But even kitchens can be great for cooking up something spicy.

You might remember the phrase "our bed is green" from the earlier chapter about play (Song of Solomon 1:16, KJV). Have you experimented yet with the great outdoors? Did you know that the stars at night really are big and bright? Trust us on this one.

Imaginative Fantasy

Esther Perel writes, "We all share a fundamental need for security, which propels us toward committed relationships in the first place; but we have an equally strong need for adventure and excitement…think about ways you might introduce risk to safety, mystery to the familiar, and novelty to the enduring."[2]

Sexual fantasies about your spouse can add adventure and excitement to play in marriage. But fantasizing about others

---

2 Esther Perel, *Mating in Captivity* (New York: Harper, 2006), 14.

invites darkness into your union, bringing distrust and division to you and the one you love. You and your mate must be sure your imaginings flow from the kingdom of light. In order to make sure this happens, ask the Holy Spirit for discernment to be sure any enticing fantasy is pleasing to God.

Some studies indicate that over 57 percent of men fantasize about others during sex with their spouse.[3] Women can be found guilty of this as well. This is dangerous—deadly dangerous—disconnecting you from the love of your partner. We want you to remain pure and devoted to your mate even in your fantasies. The goal is to connect emotionally and physically with the one with whom you share holy matrimony.

It is wise to keep some light on during sexual play, even if only a single candle. Complete darkness may seem helpful to those who are particularly shy. However, darkness can stimulate excessive fantasies in those prone to remember lovers or images from past sexual experiences. Seeing the one you are sexually enjoying increases love, appreciation, and relational bonding.

There is great value in imagination inside the safe playground of marriage. The most satisfying sex is found fully within these holy boundaries. Holy will never involve mental involvement with another individual who is not your spouse. Nor will it include actions that are painful, demeaning, or frightening.

A *sanctified imagination* is of great worth in marriage

---

3 Dr. Archibald D. Hart, *The Sexual Man* (Nashville: W. Publishing Group, 1994), 61.

because it is restrained by the wisdom of God. It is a powerful aphrodisiac that adds a wonderful dimension to lovemaking. Have you asked God to sanctify your fantasies?

> *Sexual fantasy occurring within the kingdom of light*
> *is love-centered and builds relational intimacy.*

Imagination controlled by the kingdom of darkness focuses on self and leads to isolation. Sexual bliss is found *only* in the kingdom of light. Declare with your mate that your minds will be sanctified—set apart for the glory of God. Your spouse will like it! And so will the Lord.

With your spouse, reminisce about erotic memories from your shared past. Daydream about them. Savor them in the night. Thinking of previous sexual encounters with your mate can be a healthy stimulus to desire, even during lovemaking. Remember what you enjoyed that morning together. Lean into the sensations you experienced during your play last week. The intimacies you experience with your mate in the present can be enhanced with fond memories of what you enjoyed together in the past.

God blesses both men and women in the night with the gift of erotic dreams. As with our imaginings while awake, we also ask Him to sanctify our dreams during sleep. Though sometimes embarrassing, it is good to share these dreams with your mate upon awakening. When it is agreeable to both of you, it can be great fun to act out your sexual dream later in the day.

You will be surprised how interesting and enjoyable they can be. God loves to lead you into creative and successful sex-play!

Sex Talk

Sex can be a wonderful topic of discussion between a wife and husband in marriage. But sometimes it can feel awkward to initiate sex talk. At a One Flesh marriage retreat, Dr. Paul Looney of Hidden Manna Ministries had each of us read aloud the message from a fortune cookie, then add the phrase "under the sheets" to complete the sentence. This was both fun and funny. It was amazing how suggestive these nonsexual sentences became with the addition of three short words. We all laughed till our faces turned bright red. You might want to go to a Chinese buffet tonight—then again, take-out might be a better option.

*It can be fun for lovers to tease each other
by thinking and talking sexually together.*

Sex talk with your mate is a good habit to enjoy from time to time. It can be fun—even enticing! Use your creative imagination to get past the fear and push on into this enjoyable topic of conversation. It is important to talk about sex regularly. But *don't* wear out your partner with the subject.

Talking about sex keeps the topic active in the mind of both husband and wife. When you think pleasant thoughts about sex, it increases your desire to enjoy intimate encounters together. While talking about sex, share healthy daydreams you have had about your spouse. Share these creative ideas with your mate only as suggestions to consider. No pressure.

Some friends told us they went "skinny dipping" at the beach on their honeymoon to the Bahamas. Come to think of it, though, they didn't tell us if they played while in the water. We all need a little discretion from time to time.

Talking about great sexual encounters can be the first step in the direction of yet another experience well worth remembering. Innovative sex-play can become your new normal as God leads you into amazing ways to enjoy lovemaking.

Boundaries

Sexual imaginings bring blessings to a marriage when the inspiration is from the kingdom of light. Any aspect of who we are, including our sexual creativity, can be dangerous when directed by darkness. Sadly, the dark side of imagination is sometimes not fully revealed until *after* the marriage begins. The following true story illustrates this point.

Newlyweds Joseph and Abigail came to us in distress. Neither of them had been able to fully engage in sex. They were young, healthy, and in love, but their lovemaking was simply not sizzling. They were disappointed and ready to make some changes that would enable them to be expert lovers.

Piercing questions revealed past sin issues that needed to be dealt with in both Joseph and Abigail before sexual satisfaction could come. Joseph admitted a little interest in porn. The "little interest" had even manifested the previous night when he chose not to go to bed as early as Abigail. It became evident that this interest was in reality an addiction where he regularly engaged in porn. Abigail was quite sad to hear this news, but very loving and kind in her response to his asking her forgiveness.

Abigail then began her own confession. Tears flowed as she told of a brief foray into a lesbian relationship when she was in high school. She was from a small town. A girl befriended her and they began spending more and more time together. Often, they would sleep over at one another's houses on Friday nights after the high school football game. Abigail cried that she never truly wanted the gay lifestyle, but had found the intimate touch very appealing. Now as a married woman, each time she and Joseph made love she felt shame and grief from her past sin. With hugs and tears Joseph forgave his bride.

That evening the Holy Spirit came in a strong and powerful way. Joseph asked God to forgive him and told the mean spirit of sexual perversion/porn to leave. It did! Then we prayed for Jesus to renew Joseph's mind. Abigail followed suit and was swiftly forgiven and delivered from her sin. The shame left as she realized the power of bringing things done in darkness into the light of Jesus.

At the close of the evening, we prayed with them, asking Jesus to sanctify their imaginations, to make *every* sexual image in their minds clean and holy. Weeks after this evening of prayer and counsel, they happily reported fully enjoying each other without further shame or dark imaginings. Today they have a beautiful baby and a lovely marriage.

Jesus is the Redeemer. He has redeemed us from the many sins we have committed. And He can redeem you too. Joseph and Abigail overcame the devil by the word of their testimony and the blood of the Lamb (Revelation 12:10).

If any shame or darkness in your past is dampening sexual enjoyment in your marriage, Jesus is the answer.

Find a trusted pastor to talk and pray with you for forgiveness, cleansing, and renewal. God wants you to be free and safe and innocent in your playground.

Do the two of you long to frolic in delicious sexual pleasure? Through your sanctified imaginations God can lift your lovemaking to a passionate level beyond your wildest dreams. He delights in surprising you. Just ask Him!

DR. DAN'S PRESCRIPTIONS FOR IMAGINE

* Pray together, asking the Holy Spirit to take over your imaginations that they may become sanctified tools for making love.
* Daydream about creative ways to enjoy each other's bodies through touch, taste, and smell.
* Scheme together in planning an out-of-the-ordinary playdate. Anticipating a sexual encounter can be very provocative.

7

Satisfy

Michelle freely talked about her young adult years of promiscuity. She had many sexual partners—some thrills and occasional excitement, but very little satisfaction. Michelle often told us how she did not feel loved; there had been so many disappointments from her lovers. She had been lied to. She had been cheated on. She felt used and abused. Then her world changed.

One day while working in a rehabilitation hospital, Michelle met the man of her dreams. Jeff was smart and handsome. He was witty. He was kind. He was also a quadriplegic. Jeff spent his days in a wheelchair, unable to move from his neck down. Their relationship progressed rapidly, and soon they married.

Michelle was happy to help with Jeff's physical needs. He fully met her emotional needs, and she was quick to say that Jeff really loved her. He told her she was beautiful, he enjoyed watching her walk by, and he was a great kisser. He stimulated her and satisfied her. He proved to her again and again that lovemaking is far more than intercourse. Love never fails.

What Is Satisfaction?

Can sex by itself bring satisfaction to a couple through years of being together? As Michelle learned the hard way before meeting Jeff, the answer is no.

> *Like M&M's®, good sex can be enjoyable*
> *time and time again. But why settle for M&M's®*
> *when you can have fine chocolate?*

Great sex can be so delightfully delicious that it satiates the soul. What does it really mean when marriage partners say that they are sexually satisfied?

Satisfaction can be defined as contentment derived from gratifying an appetite, desire, or need. In marriage, God gives spouses an appetite for sex, and at times it can be remarkably strong. Both husband and wife desire sexual play because it is something they truly need. God's desire is that they both be *fully satisfied*.

As we shared in chapter 5, sex is designed to be a very pleasurable experience for both the husband and the wife.

The *experiences* of life can be joyful and wonderful. But the *relationships* in life are what build true contentment.

The emotional and sexual intimacies of marriage give it the potential to be the most satisfying relationship of all.

Great sex can be a catalyst for deepening the love bond between husband and wife. Sex that satisfies is not focused on *goals,* such as frequency, technique, arousal, or orgasm.

Rather, it is aimed at sharing *relational messages* that are sent and received with exuberant joy. Consider these satisfying sentiments that can be expressed through lovemaking:

- I want to please you.
- I am attracted to you and passionately desire you.
- It is fun and satisfying to be with you.
- You hold a special and unique position in my life.
- You are beautiful/handsome.
- I want to create something new and wonderful with you.
- And, most importantly, I love you!

Every sexual encounter brings an opportunity to express these thoughts with your most intimate friend.

As you bask together in the afterglow of satisfying lovemaking, there is an intense sense of peace shared by both lovers. Your bodies are sweetly relaxed. It is easy to be anxious about nothing (Philippians 4:6). You feel comforted, accepted, and loved. Your partner is blessed, joyful, and thankful. Together you have been surprised, even amazed, and totally astonished once again. Your cups overflow with love (Psalm 23:5).

Satisfying sex is a *supernatural gift* to marriage. These intimate moments produce joyful memories that extend blessings for years to come. This is not the fleeting enjoyment of purely physical sex. It is a powerful encounter building a rich, meaningful, and lasting union between two who are one flesh.

Standing Stones

Remember the fine chocolates we talked about above? We love to share these together, feeding them to each other in a slow and seductive way. Every morsel is savored as we eat these treats with the maximum possible pleasure. Great sex should also be *savored*—in the afterglow as you embrace one another, then again and again as you reminisce about it through the years.

The Israelites knew how to preserve their favorite memories. Their common practice was to erect *standing stones* to celebrate special events that were worth remembering. For example, the Bible says, "Then Samuel took a stone and set it up between Mizpah and Shen. He named it Ebenezer, saying, 'Thus far has the LORD helped us'" (1 Samuel 7:12).

You remember that time. Yes, *that* time…the setting, the special closeness, the really strong "O," the sex-play imprinted in your mind, with sensations you can almost feel when you recall them. The unforgettable event that makes both of you smile when it is mentioned is a *sexual standing stone*.

Celebrate particularly satisfying encounters as victories in your marriage. It can be fun having pet words for each particular sexual standing stone. You two can mention it even in a group with no one but you knowing what in the world you are talking about. These gifts from God can be savored over and over again.

Why not decide to pursue yet another sexual standing stone? Plan a sexual getaway (even in your own home) with the intent of experiencing something sensational. No sexual gymnastics are required.

*The goal is for both you and your partner to feel
cherished as you sensually enjoy one another.*

Begin your time together by talking about great sex you've enjoyed in the past. Reminiscing can be the first step toward yet another unforgettable encounter.

Lovemaking Sentence Stems

Have you ever completed sexual sentence stems together? With sentence stems you take turns completing the phrase, answering quickly with the first thought that pops into your mind. These quick responses prompt a heartfelt response versus a more thought-out, careful answer. It is best for one person to begin the stems with the partner answering each, and then later changing roles. This helps ensure that the second one answering is still a bit unguarded.

You will discover other sexual sentence stems you want to employ, but we will offer a few to get you started. A fair warning: some might be blush-worthy.

- I remember the first time we…
- My favorite place we ever played was…
- The most surprising thing you ever did to me was…
- I love it when you…
- Someday I want to…
- Do you remember when you wore…
- It felt so good when we…
- I felt so loved when you…

Seven Tips for Sexual Satisfaction

Thinking and talking about sexual satisfaction has been great fun! But how do you *do* what it takes to satisfy your lover? And what are the best ways your partner can satisfy you? We discussed the technical aspects of sex in chapter 5. Knowing how to arouse each other will certainly bring pleasure to both husband and wife.

Would you like to gleefully go far past sensuality, all the way to extreme satisfaction? Let us share with you seven tips that will propel you toward this wonderful, attainable goal.

Tip #1: Being one in the Spirit optimizes sexual satisfaction.

We received a charming e-mail from a friend who made a delightful discovery. She had an amazing encounter with her husband during a spiritual fast. She wrote:

> God has really been moving on Randy's heart during my fast. He prayed so beautifully for us, our family, for a home, for wisdom—with heartfelt sincerity and vulnerability for forty-five minutes! I was astounded. I just wept quietly as I listened and heard my husband maturing spiritually and growing into a beautiful, godly man. It was so *sexy*! LOL! I tell ya, there is nothing better than having your husband lead you into godliness through a humble heart!

Through this joyful experience, Jody observed that spiritual connection between spouses increase their desire for sex.

More importantly, she was soon to experience that *being one in the Spirit optimizes sexual satisfaction.*

One in the Spirit. What in the world does that mean, and how could it possibly have anything to do with our sex lives?

God loves it when both partners in marriage pursue Him. Nothing is more fun or satisfying than embracing the Spirit together.

As we pursue God together, He changes us, making us more joyful, more playful, and more sensitive. Embracing the Holy Spirit together makes us feel vibrantly alive. And, trust us, this carries over into the marriage playground as well. Sex becomes more joyful and satisfying. We guarantee that it will also become more frequent.

Tip #2: Timing can open the door to fully enjoying sex.

"Timing is everything." Well, it may not be *everything* regarding sexual satisfaction, but timing *is* a critical component of successful lovemaking. If men and women had the same patterns of sexual desire, it would be easy to know when it was best to have sex. But it is not that simple.

On any given day, a man may be amorous while his wife is not. This means neither that his libido is inappropriately high nor that hers is inadequate. Similarly, it is normal that on some days the woman might be more interested in sex than her husband. Some asymmetry in the sexual desires of marital partners is nearly always present.[1] With most couples, it

---

1   Dan and Linda Wilson, *7 Secrets of a Supernatural Marriage: The Joy of Spirit-Led Intimacy* (Racine, WI: Broadstreet Publishing, 2014), 136.

is clear that one partner (HI) desires sexual play more frequently than the other (LO), which is a common obstacle to sexual satisfaction.

Working through this difference may seem at times to be an insurmountable challenge. Truthfully, God designed the sexual libido in each of us with perfect wisdom and purpose. Though varied, each level of desire is part of His perfect plan. Overcoming the challenge of HI versus LO is an opportunity for you to show love by adapting to the needs of your lover.

Timing can open the door to fully enjoying sex. The patience required for the best timing is one of the fruit of the Spirit that God places in our hearts (Galatians 5:22–23). The needed wisdom is also given to us directly by God (Proverbs 1:6). So what do we do? Compromise! When HI waits patiently for the time that LO is most receptive, and LO wisely plays a bit more often to please HI, the results are beyond amazing.

This is consistent with Paul's command in Philippians 2:3–4: "Do nothing out of selfish ambition or vain conceit, but in humility consider others better than yourselves. Each of you should look not only to your own interests, but also to the interests of others."

Mutual selflessness is a key to sexual fulfillment.

Tip #3: The Golden Rule of sexual satisfaction.

Sarah really enjoyed having her husband, Greg, hold her. His embrace made her feel loved and special. She liked playing with him, loved giving him "O's," but rarely did she reach orgasm. Greg had always wanted Sarah to like sex as much as he did. He knew he *needed* sexual release a few times each week. He trusted her that she truly was happy helping him climax. After a few years of marriage, however, the Holy Spirit changed Greg's heart. Although he still wanted *his* sexual appetite satiated, it became his priority to give love to Sarah— at the times and in the ways that were best for *her*. He had discovered the secret of satisfying both of them.

Sarah had always been willing to have sex when Greg was ready, even when she was not in the mood. But when he would wait until *she* was receptive, they were *both* glad they had delayed. His focus was now to satisfy her needs each day, whether or not they shared sexual play.

Soon Sarah learned how to relax and truly enjoy their sexual encounters. She discovered that she could be naked and unashamed. Freedom reigned. Sarah could now accept, and even pursue, the intense sensations of Greg pleasuring *her*. She loved the ways he could make her toes tingle. And, much to both Greg and Sarah's delight, she began to orgasm frequently.

Greg learned and implemented the Golden Rule: he learned to do unto Sarah *as* he would have her do to him. Laughingly they tell us that they enjoy sex much more now since learning that they *both* need sexual release. The Holy Spirit has brought freedom and satisfaction to their marriage bed.

Tip #4: Successful lovemaking begins in the mind.

Frequently the woman has a lower libido than the man. Yet it is not uncommon that she is HI and he is LO. Regardless of who is lower, there is great value in submitting to the sexual needs of the higher partner—not every time requested, but more often than might naturally be desired.

> *Sex on a regular basis often increases awareness*
> *and interest, particularly when offered as a gift*
> *of love to the partner with the higher desire.*

Successful lovemaking begins in the mind. LO needs to consciously make the effort to be interested more often than might come naturally. This blesses HI as a way of saying, "I love you." Thinking about sex with your lover will increase your desire and lead to improved satisfaction for both of you.

If you are HI, submit to LO's lower libido by patiently waiting for your partner to be more interested and available. It is wise to flirt gently on the lowest of days. Listen to your mate's words. Observe body language. Consider the responses to your friendly flirts. God will give you wisdom to know both how and when to best love your lover.

HI should *always* be receptive if LO is interested in play. Do not miss this exquisite opportunity! Encourage LO to express desire when it comes. This is good news for both of you! HI must be patient, allowing the frequency of sex to be below his or her ideal. Delayed gratification is a way of dying to self and showing love to your lover. It says, "You are more important to me than sex. It is my desire to pay attention to your desires in our lovemaking."

Regardless of whose sexual drive is higher or lower, these

same basic principles apply. Sexual satisfaction within a marriage requires *both* HI and LO to submit to the needs of their partner. Sex is a two-way street, which means the value of submission runs in both directions.

> *The goal is to lovingly coax each other into middle ground where wife and husband can enjoy playing at a frequency pleasing to both.*

HI and LO can change places over time, a reversing of roles through the seasons of our lives. "If one falls down, the other can pick him up" (Ecclesiastes 4:10, our paraphrase) can apply to sexual desire. Regardless of who is HI and who is LO, focus on ways to lift your partner up through love. We are confident you will both be blessed.

Tip #5: Sex is more satisfying when it is regularly enjoyed.

God has never been reluctant to talk about sex. He has strong opinions on the subject and freely shares them with us throughout Scripture. For example, Paul writes:

The husband should fulfill his marital duty to his wife, and likewise the wife to her husband. The wife's body does not belong to her alone but also to her husband. In the same way, the husband's body does not belong to him alone but also to his wife. Do not deprive each other except by mutual consent and for a time, so that you may devote yourselves to prayer. Then come together again so that Satan will not tempt you because of your lack of self-control (1 Corinthians 7:3–5).

In a healthy marriage, spouses choose to love one another every day. To keep the marriage vital and alive, it is very important that we also choose to show that love often through some form of sexual play.

Sex is more satisfying when it is regularly enjoyed.

Paul wrote, "Then come together again so that Satan will not tempt you." Does this sound like a command? At the very least it is wise instruction from our God. After an extended period of inactivity, when sexual interest may be low, intentional lovers simply decide to be intimate. Purpose to play! It is amazing how valuable and pleasurable this kind of lovemaking can be.

Tip #6: Love your mate by giving them all of who you are.

Toward the end of His time on the earth, Jesus told His disciples, "My command is this: Love each other as I have loved you. Greater love has no one than this, that he lay down his life for his friends" (John 15:12–13). Love each other. That sounds like something fun husbands and wives would want to do. But laying down your life sounds much, much harder. Your "life" includes all of who you are. And *all* is exactly what is required of you.

Every part of who you are—body, soul, and spirit—can be

used by God to bless your partner in marriage. Their desires and needs are of immense importance to you. Fulfill them. Don't hold back. *Love your mate by giving them all of who you are.* Then they can, in turn, respond by giving all of themselves to you.

Jesus modeled this by laying down His life so that we might find it. Yes, this also applies to our lovemaking where we lay down our lives for our closest and dearest friend—our spouse. This truly is satisfying!

Tip #7: Sexual satisfaction comes easier when you both feel loved.

One of the Pharisees tested Jesus by asking Him which commandment was the greatest. Jesus replied, "'Love the Lord your God with all your heart and with all your soul and with all your mind.' This is the first and greatest commandment. And the second is like it: '*Love your neighbor as yourself*'" (Matthew 22:37–39).

Your spouse is your nearest neighbor whom you are commanded to love. Love him. Love her. While you are at it, don't forget to love yourself in the process. You must have a healthy self-image before you will be able to love your neighbor "as yourself."

You and your partner are of great value, co-heirs with Christ (Romans 8:17) and ambassadors in the kingdom of God (2 Corinthians 5:20). You are the recipients of love from God Himself. We love because He first loved us (1 John 4:19).

Complete the love cycle by sharing it with one another. Sex, you will have noticed, is a wonderful way for this love to flow. You will be so glad you loved well when love boomerangs back to you! *Satisfaction with sex comes easier when you both feel loved.*

True Satisfaction

Marriage is meant to be a demonstration of the relational intimacy present in heaven from before the beginning of time. We all want our marriages to be like "heaven on earth." Jesus prayed for the Father's will to be done "on earth as it is in heaven" (Matthew 6:10). It is God's wonderful plan that you and your mate get a taste of heaven through satisfying sexual intimacy.

Ultimately, true satisfaction from sex in marriage comes from authentic love flowing freely—day in and day out—permeating the relationship. Husband and wife regularly give and receive love that is genuine. Love pours in and love pours out in two directions every day of the week. Both partners are deeply loved, and both feel absolutely blessed.

This kind of love is unnatural. In fact, it is supernatural. The love we are describing throughout this book and in the context of marriage can be summed up in a single Greek word—*agape*. God is love (1 John 4:8). Yes, God is *agape*. He pours His love into our hearts by the Spirit whom He has given to us (Romans 5:5). This love, in turn, empowers us to do what is best for another instead of focusing on ourselves.

The heartbeat of heaven is agape,
*which is the supernatural key for unlocking
the door to satisfying lovemaking.*

The atmosphere of heaven can be enjoyed on earth when the *agape* of God floods through your marriage. In its flow, you can honestly love one another (John 13:34). And, in doing so, God's love is made complete (1 John 3:12). Now this is truly satisfying.

We have said it before and we'll say it again: Love is relational. It's a two-way street. You can only become an expert *lover* through relationship with an expert *lovee*. The perfect love of God in your spouse releases you to your destiny as one who gives and receives love extremely well. Sex in marriage is a celebration of a deep and lasting love between spouses—love that comes straight from the heart of God.

Knowing God deeply increases our capacity to receive His love. The Greek word *gnosko* is used many times in the New Testament to describe how God intimately knows us and we can intimately know Him. *Gnosko* is relational. It has a strong familiarity that comes only through experience—as occurs between husband and wife when they "know" each other in sexual intimacy.[2]

One example of this is John 8:32. Jesus said, "You shall *know* the truth, and the truth will make you free." Jesus is the Truth we are to know in an intimate manner. And, as a result

---

2 *Strong's Exhaustive Concordance*, s.v. "*gnōsesthe*," Greek 1097.

of that knowledge, that intimacy of knowing Him, great freedom comes. The love we share with Jesus prepares us for a satisfying love relationship in marriage.

As dearly loved children of God, we are led by His Spirit (Romans 8:14). The Holy Spirit is the best source of guidance in becoming an expert lover. Yes, listening and responding to the Spirit before and during play really does make it better. God wants us to fully enjoy sex! He created the desire and the capacity for both husband and wife to be deeply satisfied through lovemaking. The wind of the Spirit will blow us exactly where, when, and how to proceed in physical intimacy.

> *Spirit-led lovers are like fine red wine—*
> *they improve with age.*

For more than half a century it has been commonly accepted that sexual drive peaks in the late teens for men and in the thirties for women.[3] But, regardless of when these libido peaks occur, the ability to satisfy and be satisfied through sexual relations can increase for decades.

Contrary to popular opinion, young lovers are generally *not* the best lovers. The Spirit refines our skills of lovemaking throughout the years. It is recognized that happily married people in their later decades are often the most satisfied lovers. We would agree with that!

Another widely held belief is that the men and women

---

3 Alfred Kinsey, *Sexual Behavior in the Human Female* (Philadelphia: W. B. Saunders Company, 1953).

who are the most attractive will also be the most sexually satisfied in marriage. In truth, good looks have little to do with good sex. Amazing lovers come in all shapes and sizes.

In her book, *Good Girl's Guide to Great Sex*, Sheila Wray Gregoire substantiates our beliefs. She states,

> The women who had the most fun in the bedroom were not the Paris Hiltons of the world. The prototypical sexually happy woman better resembled that middle-aged secretary who lives down your street, puttering around in her garden, packing an extra twenty-five pounds. Gravity has taken its toll, but she's the one who's the tiger in the bedroom. She's the one having fun, because she has the secret to sexual success: she's been married to the same man for the last twenty-two years, and they're totally and utterly committed to one another.[4]

Sheila goes on to say,

> We feel the best and have the best sex when we are in committed marriages that we know are for life. Conservative religious women tend to be in those types of relationships. They take marriage seriously, as do their husbands. So they feel the most cherished and the most loved. And hence they experience the most fireworks.

---

4   Sheila Wray Gregoire, *The Good Girl's Guide to Great Sex* (Grand Rapids: Zondervan, 2012), 16.

For women, commitment is the best aphrodisiac, far better than Botox, breast enlargements, or sex toys.[5]

Enjoy being that tiger in the bedroom! Learn from our tips and follow the doctor's orders—Dr. Dan's prescriptions. You will be well on your way to becoming the "greatest lover on earth" for your spouse.

DR. DAN'S PRESCRIPTIONS FOR SATISFY

* Surprise your wife with a nice dinner date without it being a special occasion.
* At naptime, use your husband's tummy or chest as your pillow.
* Picnic by the fireplace. Enjoy the food, and then enjoy each other.

---

5 Ibid., 31.

#

8

I t is commonly said that the only thing constant in life is change. But did you ever consider that statement as applying to sex? John and Karen have been very transparent with us concerning their sexual adaptations.

During the early years of their marriage, John and Karen happily used oral contraceptives. They wanted to really enjoy each other without the fear of premature pregnancy. With time they chose when they would try to conceive, and were happily blessed with a couple of great kids. Life was good. It was the perfect time for John to have the big "V." Yes, he bravely had a vasectomy.

Then their sexual world shifted. Through Bible study, prayer, and counsel from some close friends, Karen became convinced that God should be their family planner, not them. And John agreed. His vasectomy was reversed. Babies began coming in regular two-year intervals. Many babies! All single births.

In their early forties, Karen and John were really tired from all the stresses of pregnancies and babies, along with managing school activities with kids in many grade levels. Life was exhausting. Together they entered a serious time of prayer and fasting, asking the Holy Spirit for direction about family planning at this stage of life. They received perfect peace from the Lord that it was fine with Him if they once again used contraceptives.

"To everything there is a season," the Bible says (Ecclesiastes 3:1, NKJV). God is not alarmed when we need to consult Him with the same question at different times throughout our lives. Mysteriously, He is the same yesterday, today, and forever, while at the same time His mercies are new every morning (Hebrews 13:8; Lamentations 3:23).

> *Be willing to adapt with your lover*
> *as the seasons of life change.*

Good Compromise

Karen and John adjusted successfully to sexual challenges in their marriage. They made compromises—not the bad kind that tear down integrity, but the good kind that build character. Healthy compromise involves both partners sacrificing a current, personal choice that is good, and moving on to a new choice that is best. *The goal of compromise is to bless the marriage.* Each spouse intends the adjustment to be a sign of love to the other and evidence of their belief that the joint decisions are best for the vitality of the relationship.

The result of a good compromise is much better than if either spouse had "won" in making the decision. Victory and defeat in a marriage relationship is not good for either partner. And capitulation is almost never wise. By working together, a helpful adjustment is made through wisdom and love.

In *all* marriages, couples need good compromises as they adjust to one another's styles of sexual play. Isn't it fun to explore together? And isn't it astonishing that there is always more to discover even after many years of marriage? It is also delightful that what works really well one day is not necessarily the best on another playdate. No, no, no—we should never be stuck in a dull rut! It sucks life from you! Common ground, where both lovers are adapting through compromise, is the place where great sexual pleasure can be found.

Some adaptation will be invaluable in the following aspects of sensuality:

- Type of seduction: is today's seduction to be subtle or unmistakably overt?
- Length of foreplay: shall it be short and sweet, or longer and savored?
- Sources of stimulation: fingers, tongue, genitals—so many choices! In fact, sometimes the combinations are nice.
- Body positions: are we feeling creative or is it best to be traditionally conservative this time?
- Lighting: dark, dim, or bright—which best fits her mood tonight?
- Nudity: covered or exposed—believe it or not, men often prefer a little lace to peek through.
- Visual arousal: is it of minor or major importance during this playtime?

- Speed of arousal: savoring or accelerated—slow cooker or microwave version?
- High plateau: repeated or pushing through—is it best to keep your lover high, almost maddeningly high for a while, or quickly give them the big "O" they are wanting?
- Timing: morning, afternoon, evening, or middle of the night—yes! Yes!

Arousal Challenges

There are many challenges to sexual arousal in lovemaking. Occasionally, both husbands and wives face physical, emotional, and spiritual issues that can drain desire and reduce their responses. It is helpful to be aware that these are common. The good news is that facing challenges raises the level of oxytocin in the brain.[1] And remember that bonding occurs when oxytocin flows.

Bonding! Your relationship will flourish as you continue loving each other. With some Spirit-led *adaptation*, you will overcome these problems.

Ladies First

It is not unusual that a woman is challenged by libido that is lower than she and her husband desire. In all honesty, initial

---

1 "How to make stress your friend," Kelly McGonigal, video at TEDGlobal 2013, filmed June 2013, www.ted.com/talks/kelly_mcgonigal_how_to_make_stress_your_friend (accessed 2/26/2015).

sexual encounters are often not very pleasurable for women. The vaginal stretching, the messiness—both can be unpleasant.

Arousal is a learned response that takes time to develop. In the early years, both husband and wife may lack the lovemaking skills required to ensure arousal for her. This is not at all uncommon. Patience promotes success in sexual play. Did you know that libido *and* capacity for arousal could increase markedly when they are actively pursued? Now that is good news!

Sexual interest varies dramatically with hormonal levels during the menstrual cycle too. A few days each month can be predictably void of desire. The busyness of life can rob the most amorous wife of her interest in sex. And fatigue is the enemy of romance. Sometimes couples must admit it is simply *not* a good day to play.

Husbands, be sensitive to the moods and needs of your wife. Wait for signs that she is receptive before shifting your advances into high gear. Ask God for wisdom to recognize when opportunity for intimacy knocks again.

Delaying gratification can lead to an encounter that is really satisfying.

Some wives may have high interest and pleasure in sex, but still have great difficulty achieving orgasm. Ten percent of women say they have never experienced sexual climax.[2] This inability to orgasm is known as ***anorgasmia***.

---

2 The Society of Obstetricians and Gynaecologists of Canada, "Female Orgasms: Myths and Facts," http://sogc.org/publications/female-orgasms -myths-and-facts/, (accessed 11/ 1/2014).

Orgasms become more frequent for women after several years of marriage when they feel safe and secure in a stable, loving relationship. Leaning into the pleasurable sensations of arousal, her first "O" may come unexpectedly with overwhelming intensity. As she learns to savor these delightful feelings, they can be enjoyed more and more over time.

Unfortunately, ***dyspareunia*** (pain with intercourse) is a common problem for women. The first sexual encounter including penile penetration is often painful due to vaginal stretching and tearing of the hymen. Frequent sex-play can lead to irritation and bruising of the genitals, both his and hers. Infections and other sources of chronic inflammation can also be contributing factors to this pain. In some cases, a physical cause for the pain cannot be found.

The male students in my (Dan's) medical school would joke about this problem saying, "Dyspareunia is better than no-eunia." Wives and husbands whose sexual pleasure is limited by vaginal pain would agree that this is not a joking matter. When discomfort persists, medical evaluation is recommended. Occasionally psychological and spiritual counseling are helpful as well.

Pregnancy brings a plethora of challenges to the marital bed. Hormonal changes dramatically alter emotions, libido, and bodily responses. As the baby grows, a woman's shape is altered in ways that may make her feel unattractive and can physically block favorite positions of lovemaking. Although *her* desire for sex may be lowered, *his* remains the same. This is an excellent time to practice good compromising skills, while remembering that "love is patient, love is kind" (1 Corinthians 13:4).

Men's Hurdles

Men have their own set of hurdles that must be overcome to fully enjoy the playground of marriage. During his first sexual encounters, it is common for a young husband to climax very quickly after intercourse begins. This ***premature ejaculation*** allows little time for his wife to enjoy her sexual experience. When this happens, do not despair. Use the challenge of climaxing too early as an opportunity to bless your lover. Spend *lots* of time pleasuring your wife before and after you are quickly satisfied. Techniques to delay ejaculation can be found on the Internet. It can be fun to read these together as a couple and discover what works for you. Be encouraged by knowing this will gradually improve with time.

When I (Dan) turned forty, my dad tried to loan me a Viagra tie to wear to a hospital staff meeting one night. Linda laughingly refused to allow it, saying, "No way, José!" ***Erectile dysfunction*** (ED, impotence), the inability to obtain and maintain an erection long enough to enjoy sexual intercourse, affects many men in midlife and beyond. Sorry, guys. It is not a matter of *if* but *when* this will happen to every sexually active man.

There are many physical causes of ED—fatigue, side effects of medication, diabetes, heart conditions, and other forms of disease. It can be the direct result of surgical procedures, particularly a prostatectomy. Mental contributors are equally important. Depression and lagging sexual confidence join hand-in-hand as causes of this frustrating condition.

Male orgasmic disorder (MOD) is similar in its causes to ED. This is the inability to reach orgasm after a reasonable length of genital stimulation. Interestingly, as with other forms of sexual dysfunction, failure to climax is considered *normal* until it occurs in more than 25 percent of sexual attempts.[3]

Hypoactive sexual desire (low libido) can occur in husbands with its causes much the same as described in women. In some cases, a low level of the hormone testosterone (produced in the testicles and adrenal glands) can result in this disorder. Warning: Do not diagnose and treat low testosterone on your own. This diagnosis must never be assumed until medically proven with blood tests. Over-the-counter medications for this are rarely beneficial.

As in all things, God can work ED, MOD, and low libido in men for the good of couples who love Him (Romans 8:28). After experiencing any or all of these challenges, men become much more empathetic when their wives are not easily aroused. A little understanding can go a long way in helping couples get over sexual hurdles.

Overcoming Obstacles

Sexual obstacles are overcome when lovers join together to defeat them. Both you and your mate have a *need* for sexual

---

3 "What Are Male Sexual Problems," WebMD: www.webmd.com/sexual
-conditions/understanding-male-sexual-problems-basics (accessed 10/16/
2014).

pleasure. But your goal is much more than arousal and climax. Neither intercourse nor orgasm is required.

True love is the source of lasting satisfaction.

Still, libido adds life to your sex-play together. What can be done to increase passionate desire?

Indulging your five senses in nonsexual ways can prime them for later use in lovemaking. Be prepared for intimate opportunities to come by being sensual *all* the time. Listen to soothing music. Enjoy the smell of a scented candle. Admire a bright yellow rose in the garden. Savor the taste and texture of biting into a crisp apple. Sense the rush of cool water across your neck as you dive into a pool. *Everyday sensuality* increases desire for intimacy, improving responsiveness when sex is later enjoyed.

Physical health also enhances libido in both husbands and wives. Enjoy a healthy diet. Indulge in an occasional nap. Exercise regularly with your lover and best friend. Just being together increases the sense of intimacy between mates. Keep moving, but the exercise does not have to be vigorous. Motion makes you feel more alive inside, and exertion increases blood flow to *all* your body parts.

Sadly, abuse experienced previously by one or both partners is a common obstacle faced in marriage. Whether physical, mental, emotional, or sexual, these are gut-wrenching memories. You might wonder, "Can God overcome something as awful as this?" The answer is yes! God is far bigger than any challenge you have experienced.

Astonishing healing can be received through kindness, sensitivity, patience, and prayer. And, yes, time can bring much relief too. Prayer ministry for inner healing or deliverance may be required in order to experience that relief. Forgiveness is absolutely essential. A trusted pastor or Christian counselor will be able to offer wise counsel for *both* of you—any abuse affecting one partner in reality affects both the husband and wife. You can trust the Holy Spirit to have the solution. Victory is at hand!

Ill but Interested

We had been married a few years, had a toddler, and were eight months pregnant with our second son. Out of the blue one morning I (Dan) awoke in excruciating pain, so intense that I could hardly walk. Tests revealed that I had serious lower back problems—a herniated lumbar-sacral disc with bulging discs at higher spinal levels. Conservative treatment while we awaited the birth of our baby did nothing to alleviate the pain. Back surgery was required when our son was only one month old.

The lumbar and sacral nerves go to the most important of the erogenous zones. Although slim, there was a risk of my losing the ability to play sexually. And there were other fears to overcome as well. After surgery I was told to do no twisting or lifting. Could we play? Should we play? Would it hurt me, even damage me, to have sex? This sudden loss of physical activity also threatened my sense of manliness. Chronic pain is a real downer.

I (Linda) had my own set of issues to deal with during this intense health crisis. My hormones were in upheaval from the recent pregnancy and birth. I was exhausted from taking care of a newborn, a toddler, and an invalid husband. Fear was my biggest challenge. Dan couldn't walk without extreme discomfort. Would he ever work again? Might my weight hurt him during intercourse? How could I help him through his depression? Would life ever be "normal" again?

God is good! By His amazing grace, I (Dan) became strong enough to work again and even coached a little league baseball team. I don't run very often, but I still love to snow ski! Occasionally, we still need to be careful with our positions in sex if I get a little flare-up with sciatica, but we have been blessed in enjoying our playground!

Many illnesses bring challenges to intimacy in marriage. Diabetes can reduce the sensitivity of nerves, thereby reducing the pleasure of sensual touch. Heart disease may mix fear and fatigue in with the joys of lovemaking. Removal of ovaries can suddenly change a woman's hormonal balance, while a mastectomy and hysterectomy may alter her feelings of femininity. And men sometimes struggle with ED or MOD after prostate surgery.

Every couple deals with diseases or other issues that challenge their intimacy. Even a common cold or severe sunburn can put a damper on play. Illness is an enemy to the enjoyment of sex. Regardless of physical dysfunction, we remain sexual beings who desire and need to play. Intimacy must be adjusted at times, but the enjoyment of lovemaking never fades.

Aging Well

One day Linda was enjoying lunch with a few ladies. One of them had recently married an older man. Someone asked her what it was like having a husband twenty years older. Without blinking an eye, she quipped, "Everything is exactly the same except it takes longer."

"There is a time for everything, and a season for every activity under heaven" (Ecclesiastes 3:1). Fortunately, the season for enjoying sex is very long. Arousal in older spouses is much different from those in their twenties. As Linda learned that day, it might progress a little more slowly, but the latter years still remain a time for sexual pleasing and being pleased.

> *Satisfaction with intimacy in marriage does not need to go down over time. Lovers often become better at making love as the decades pass.*

Many of us are overly concerned about the effects of aging on our ability to enjoy lovemaking. Movies and television generally cast older actors in the roles of those who can no longer be satisfied. Younger characters are often depicted as men and women in sexual overdrive, while the aged have no more interest in play.

We are misled into believing that those who are older have lost the ability to enjoy sexual pleasure. This is far from the truth in God's wondrous plan. Wise Solomon discovered that "the silver-haired head is a crown of glory" (Proverbs 16:31, NKJV). Each year is a gift from God. Each birthday, each anniversary, and every day we celebrate *life* with the one we love. As a matter of fact, the childbearing years involve less than half the life of long marriages. There may not be procreation in the latter years, but the fun, pleasure, and bonding of sex still remain.

Adaptive Place

Are you challenged by an illness? Less fit than you were fifty years ago? Did you know that physical impairment usually does not reduce interest in sex? Lovemaking varies greatly in different seasons of life, but satisfaction with sex never needs to end. Enjoy your sexual standing stones, but leave the past in the past. *Adapt* the ways you play to the needs of today.[4]

Be fresh. Sitting, standing, leaning, or lying down—intercourse can bring pleasure when enjoyed from any angle. If you find your "normal" positions to be unsafe or uncomfortable, read a Christian sex blog and try out some of their suggestions. While you are at it, create a few of your own.

---

4 An excellent resource for adapting sexual play can be found in your nearest nursing school library. It is a textbook entitled *Rehabilitation Nursing: Prevention, Intervention, and Outcomes* by Shirley P. Hoeman (Mosby/Elsevier Publisher, 2008). Of particular interest to our subject, we recommend pages 560–579. Another excellent resource is *Pure Eyes, Clean Heart: A Couple's Journey to Freedom from Pornography* by Jen and Craig Ferguson (Discovery House, 2014). Its points go far beyond just porn. A blog that contains really good information is *Hot, Holy, & Humorous: Sex & Marriage by God's Design:* http://hotholyhumorous.com.

Try some new ways to be one flesh with the one you love.
Being flexible at playtime is fun!

Do you have a heart condition? Are you concerned about too much exertion during sex-play? First ask your physician for approval, then concentrate on ways to have sex with minimal exertion. Side-lying positions are easier on your heart than being on top. If you're the man, stay on your back and let your wife do most of the work. She might assume a sitting position across your pelvis while you rest. You can enjoy watching, touching, and squeezing anything within reach. If you've not tried this before, you might both find it particularly pleasing, regardless of age or fitness level. And, wives, if arthritis pain affects your hips, the nesting spoon position is a good one to try with your husband entering from behind.

Digital (finger) ***stimulation*** can be very useful when intercourse is ill advised. Little effort is required when only hands are used. The results can be spectacular for both husband and wife. Let your fingers do the walking and you will only get out of breath a little bit.

For more rapid sexual arousal, oral sex can be powerfully pleasurable. Both giver and receiver can be physically relaxed while delightful sensations are enjoyed. This option should be considered but never required. If it is right for your marriage, oral stimulation can beautifully satisfy desire.

In some circumstances, masturbation can be a useful adjunct to lovemaking in marriage. With aging or illness, arousal may be difficult for one or both partners. Self-stimulation can be used concurrently with typical foreplay or intercourse to enhance sex-play. This might allow orgasm with your mate to be reached more easily.

Masturbation can be performed in view of the other spouse as a part of foreplay. If the partner can participate, they can assist by also touching erogenous zones. This can be strongly arousing for both people involved. Sometimes a husband or wife will self-stimulate in the room with their disabled spouse as a way of sharing sexual intimacy together. Thoughts should always be directed toward the partner, never pictures or people outside of the marriage.

As you know, our God is all about relationship.

If you sense that a style of play is hurting your relationship with God or your spouse in any way, it should not be a part of your lovemaking.

Devote yourselves to doing what is good—things that are excellent and profitable for everyone (Titus 3:8).

Push Through

Our bodies change. Sometimes we must literally reposition, adapting the way we play to accommodate health changes and aging. Sex can still be fantastic in the midst of physical challenges. How can we *push through* the obstacles to once again enjoy intimacy?

Begin with your mind. A common trap is to think about

your difficulties with intimacy: the obstacles and challenges, the disappointments and frustrations. What you think about is what you empower. Please do not focus on your problems. Instead, whatever is lovely, admirable, and excellent—think about these things (Philippians 4:8). Remember those sexual standing stones of the past? Plan to celebrate new ones. Yes, there will be new ones, different perhaps than in the past, but delightful nonetheless.

Recall the peace and joy of sex together when you, as a couple, were in an easier place. Those gratifying encounters from the past proclaim that your marriage will flourish in the future. Focus on the beautiful aspects of your intimacy right now. Savor the sweetness of what you have.

Seek wise counsel. You are not alone. Others have faced and surmounted this same obstacle before. There is nothing new under the sun (Ecclesiastes 1:9). Listen to those who have helped them overcome and apply what you can to your own life.

More importantly, ask the Spirit to lead you. The Counselor has the answer to every question. His ways are creative and stimulating, and He will teach you what you need to know (John 14:26).

Commit to enjoy each other in spite of all the challenges. Celebrating intimacy is beautiful. With or without an "O," lovemaking is sweet and fun. Laughingly remember "love always hopes" (1 Corinthians 13:7).

Laughter plays a vital role in lovemaking.
It really is good medicine from time to time.

In Ecclesiastes 3, Solomon told us there is a time to laugh. This Hebrew word translated as "to laugh" is *sachaq*, meaning to rejoice, to play, to be amused—it implies dancing and celebrating.[5] Certainly your relationship will benefit from a little *sachaq*, even now in this season of adjustment.

Choose. Decide. Commit to seeking intimacy. Your relationship is worth the risk. The vulnerability required in this new phase of life is somewhat like newlywed days. Early in marriage there were certainly awkward moments, some nervous giggles, a little blushing. But *nothing* kept you from trying new positions and enjoying play. Modified sex-play can become your new normal. Go for it!

Cheryl had been undergoing treatment for abdominal cancer—surgery, chemo, radiation—the works. In the midst of the treatment, she fell in love and got married. Her new husband promised to love life back into her. The physical obstacles did not alter his passion for her. The promises of God to prosper and give hope were still in effect in spite of Cheryl's health challenges (Jeremiah 29:11). Cheryl and David have now been happily married eight lovely years. And she is cancer free! They would agree with Solomon's words, "Many waters cannot quench love" (Song of Solomon 8:7).

Even now, regardless of any obstacles in your path, God wants to knock the socks off you and your mate with His

---

5 *Spirit Filled Life Bible: A Personal Study Bible Unveiling All God's Fullness in All God's Word (New King James Version)*, Jack Hayford, Ed., (Nashville: Thomas Nelson, 2002), 848.

amazing, abundant goodness. Adapting to sexual challenges is a privilege, an adventure that brings joy, laughter, and true satisfaction. It is a wonderful opportunity for you to show and to share love with your life-partner. Forever.

DR. DAN'S PRESCRIPTIONS FOR ADAPT

* Cuddle closely in bed as you pray before going to sleep.
* If either of you are feeling disconnected, snuggle with the husband's face against his wife's breast. Or find another position that will awaken your spirits and increase oneness.
* In front of your hubby, spread coconut oil slowly around your breasts. Then use more as a lubricant during foreplay and intercourse.
* Have some fun experimenting with creative sexual play and positions that work best for your need to adapt.

9

Embrace

"All tangled in a big messy knot." That is how Rebecca described herself prior to her marriage with Gabe. Most people would agree with her when looking at her life. At a young age, her mom had abandoned her, and subsequently died before having any reconciliation with Rebecca. Her dad had a string of lovers flowing in and out of the home, while also drinking away much of his income, leaving Rebecca and the other children poorly clothed and often hungry.

Feeling lost and hopeless, Rebecca met Jesus during her teen years. Her life now had meaning and purpose. She no longer felt alone. God became life to her. She felt secure and at peace with the Lord, yet she remained aloof and untrusting in relationships with other people.

Gabe unsettled her. He was a man after God's own heart. Everything he did revolved around his desire to see others discover this amazing God for themselves. He treated Rebecca with kindness. He invited her to prayer and worship meetings. He pursued her. And she eventually allowed him to catch her, although she gave him multiple opportunities to turn away—drama, tears, fear. She even took him to meet her dysfunctional family.

After marriage Rebecca noticed the knot untangling. Amazingly, she was living out the mystery of two becoming one. Laughingly, one day she said, "Two really do become one flesh!" With tremendous excitement she shared how during sex with Gabe she felt whole and at peace with herself, with God, and with the world. Jesus was healing first one heart wound, then another. Two really are better than one (Ecclesiastes 4:9)!

> *We all have pain and injury in our past—*
> *tangles in our lives. But Jesus is willing and able to*
> *restore everything to its proper place once again.*

As Rebecca discovered, He often uses sexual relations in marriage as a significant part of the healing process. We are embracing Him as we embrace one another through sexual intimacy.

Our friend JoAnn McFatter sings about this healing in her song entitled "Untangled."

I've got you where I want you,
I've got you surrounded by my love,
I've got you where I want you.
Let me hover, let me surround you with my, my jealous,
    my jealousy.
I want to detangle some things…tangled up in your heart.
I just wanna hover over you…till you see and you believe.
All I ever wanted is you…all I ever wanted is your heart.

Let me come in and hover with my Spirit…and just do
a little rearranging.[1]

Sex-play in marriage—man and woman cooperating with
each other and the Holy Spirit—is often a powerful force bringing healing to the wounds of the past. Through sex we have
an opportunity to feel calm, peaceful, secure, comforted, and
deeply loved. As husbands and wives become one with their
partners, they gain access to a wellspring of healing, a reser-
voir of wholeness. The love of God flows freely from one to the
other, rearranging and untangling the disorder in their hearts.

Embrace God

During lovemaking in holy matrimony, we are given a taste
of the glory experienced in heaven. Where two come together
in Jesus' name, He promises to be there with them (Matthew
18:20). Yes, even during lovemaking. And through His glorious presence *healing* comes.

Embracing God and each other, husband and wife receive:

- Peace: Jesus is the Prince of Peace (Isaiah 9:6).
- Joy: the joy of the Lord is our strength (Nehemiah 8:10).
- Comfort: He is the God of all comfort (2 Corinthi-
  ans 1:3).
- Relief from anxiety: do not be anxious about any-
  thing (Philippians 4:6).

1 Steve Swanson, JoAnn McFatter, Julie Meyer, and Steve Mitchell, "Untangled," *Chosen: You Are My Desire*, executively produced by Supernatural
   Marriage Ministries, 2012. Used by permission.

- Healing: it is the Lord who heals you (Exodus 15:26).

Rebecca embraced God. So did Gabe. They both wanted their love relationship to thrive. And both wisely insisted that *God had to come first.* Following what Jesus called the greatest commandment, Rebecca and Gabe loved the Lord as the primary focus of their lives (Matthew 22:37–38). Proper order brings healing, enhances romance, and leads to marital satisfaction.

God wants your marriage to be healthy and whole, a blissful experience in which *all* of your needs are met.

Your sexual longing is designed to be satisfied when you and your mate encounter the indescribable pleasure of making love. Embrace God. The psalmist declared, "Take delight in the Lord, and he will give you the desires of your heart" (Psalm 37:4).

Embrace Your Mate

Are you a good hugger? In the movies we often see passionate hugs ending with a steamy kiss, the woman's knee bent with her stiletto heel slipping off her foot. Romance! Big bear hugs are really fun too. Long, slow embraces with your lover are pretty amazing. Even a quick caress as you pass your mate in a crowded room is really nice. But embracing your spouse is much more than physical touch.

Appreciating your lover's character and integrity is part of embracing him or her as a person, as an individual.

You are both made in the image of God.
His greatest attributes can be discovered in
your mate if you are looking for them.

Recognizing your lover's true beauty does the same. Mark and Grace Driscoll go so far as to say that "your standard of beauty is your spouse."[2] No one else can even compete as the object of your affection. "You are altogether beautiful, my darling; there is no flaw in you" (Song of Solomon 4:7). Your eyes are open to reality, yet you see him or her as they truly are—absolutely gorgeous.

As you embrace your partner, also support them in realizing dreams. In the midst of obtaining a graduate degree and having a second baby, one young man had a dream of running a marathon. His sweet wife did everything she could to support him—giving up many Saturdays and evenings for his hours and hours of training, preparing his food to follow the suggested eating plan, massaging his sore muscles, *and* meeting him at the finish line with kids in tow. Bethany certainly embraced Matt's dream of being a marathoner.

Appreciate your wife's gifts. She has talents and abilities that are uniquely hers. Celebrate your husband's abilities. He should be your hero. Everyone needs pats on the back and recognition for things well done. *And your mate especially needs to hear these affirmations from you.*

---

2 Mark and Grace Driscoll, *Real Marriage: The Truth About Sex, Friendship, and Life Together* (Nashville: Thomas Nelson, 2012), 109.

Do you show honor to your lover in public? How about in private?

> *Watch your mate stand taller when they overhear*
> *you honoring them to a friend. When your spouse*
> *knows that you love and honor them, it will certainly*
> *carry over into your bedroom.*

Value the plans God has for each of you, *and* the plans He has for you as a couple. It can be very fun and exciting to embrace each other as you pray, asking the Lord to show you His plans for you as a couple. Have you tried this? He will surely delight you when you do so. Pursuing your destiny as a couple certainly increases intimacy. Running together with God might even be considered an aphrodisiac! Life with the Lord is full of adventure.

Embrace Lovemaking

Often, when talking with singles, we hear the longing in their hearts for finding the one—the special one God has set apart just for them. The longing is for oneness, completion, wholeness. In lovemaking, we all have this desire fulfilled. Are you ready to embrace lovemaking?

God created us, both male and female, with the desire to pursue sexual encounters and the capacity to thoroughly enjoy them. We believe God laughs with couples who enjoy ridiculously good sex in marriage. He has given us these gifts and is blessed when we use them well.

God wants your marriage to flourish and your sex life to sizzle.

Anyone can have sex, but lovemaking is reserved for those who have a lifelong commitment to love and be loved—by God and by the one we have chosen for keeps.

It really does remind us of Eden, and it fills our hearts with longing for the new Eden, the new Jerusalem, when heaven will be fully manifested on earth. Until then, we get to practice love.

Practice love? You can practice piano or guitar, so why not practice love?

- Practice speaking loving words—even if they provoke a nervous giggle.
- Practice touching—gentle strokes, light tickles, holding hands.
- Practice sensuous dressing—followed later by sensuous undressing.
- Practice selflessness—surprise your mate by doing something *they* enjoy.
- Practice reading Scripture to each other—1 Corinthians 13 is a great place to start.
- Practice enjoying time together—when is the last time you visited a botanical garden or somewhere out in God's beautiful creation?
- Practice cooking together—you can even be playful with the dishwashing bubbles.

- And, speaking of bubbles…practice bathing together—don't forget behind the ears!

See, practicing love is both easy and fun. Your marriage is "till death do us part." So why not enjoy it now and through all the years you get to be married? Practice makes perfect!

Have you followed Dr. Dan's prescriptions throughout this book? This might be a good time to review them and choose one to do today. Yes, today! Surely you want to comply with the doctor's orders. And we bet you can come up with some really good prescriptions on your own. We would love to hear your holy and fun schemes!

We have heard couples freely share that really good sex was the only thing that carried them through some tough spots in their marriage. We have also conversed with some friends in full-time ministry who have wonderful marriages, but are lacking in sexual contentment. They want some spice, some zip, in their lovemaking. They all want more! We are *all* sexual beings. And sex plays a huge role in our identity as married couples.

Let's be frank. We all want to be sexy *and* satisfied. The sexual desire God placed within us is real, strong, and valuable. These urges are part of who we are. So grab hold of your libido, blessing your mate in beautiful and memorable ways. True ecstasy is not an illicit drug. You can experience this in the privacy of your own bedroom.

Lovemaking is for you. With inspiration from our astounding Holy Spirit, you and your mate can be the greatest lovers on earth! Run to the farthest boundaries of your marital playground. Enjoy creative play!

> *When you love your partner freely and fully,*
> *you are bringing joy to the heart of God.*

Great sex is far bigger than just the two of you. You are a chosen people (1 Peter 2:9). In part, this means your lives should look different—and they can. Your children, your neighbors, and your coworkers will see the twinkle in your eyes and sense the contentment in your souls. They will see that you are vibrantly alive and truly in love. Your marriage will be a lighthouse in the world that is declaring the goodness of the Lord.

DR. DAN'S PRESCRIPTIONS FOR EMBRACE

- A "style show" with new underwear can turn into an enjoyable premier performance.
- July 14 is National Nude Day. Hmmm!
- Splurge on the calories, and enjoy a big, chocolate sundae together. Chocolate syrup isn't just for ice cream anymore!

10

Love

Giving and receiving love is an essential part of being a person created in the image of the Great Lover. Even tiny infants know this. When a baby is in need of love, he cries and cries until his need is met, the crying almost instantly melting away as the babe is held in his mommy's arms. And, yes, this same sweet baby gives love too. As he snuggles against his daddy's neck, his dad feels loved. As the precious little one holds a gaze with his mother, he is communicating love to her. Once again we learn the value of childlikeness in the pure and simple sharing of love.

Those who are most satisfied in their marriages have discovered a secret: Physical intimacy—lovemaking—is not about sex. It is really all about love. It really is.

Years ago I (Linda) was in desperate need of love. My dad had passed away at a young age and now my mom was dying. I kept thinking and feeling that here I was, a thirty-five-year-old orphan. I was a married woman and a mother myself, but the feelings of being orphaned were very real.

Beautifully, God showed Himself true as being a Father to the fatherless (Psalm 68:5). Yet I wanted and needed physical, tangible love. Dan, my darling friend, was able to give it to me. I would cry, and he would hold me. I could gaze into his eyes and see love reciprocated. I could snuggle against his warm chest to feel safe. And, yes, he would give me the gift of loving, comforting sex each time I needed it, expecting nothing in return. Dan loved life back into me.

Love, Love, Love

Having sex and making love are often used synonymously.

*Anyone can have sex, but true lovemaking
requires intimate connection with God,
who is the only source of true love.*

How can we describe this love? A popular passage of Scripture used at many weddings to talk about love is 1 Corinthians 13:4–8. Paul writes,

Love is patient, love is kind. It does not envy, it does not boast, it is not proud. It is not rude, it is not self-seeking, it is not easily angered, it keeps no record of wrongs. Love does not delight in evil but rejoices with the truth. It always protects, always trusts, always hopes, always perseveres. Love never fails.

This revelation from the apostle Paul on what true love looks like is not only good to consider at the start of a relationship, but it is absolutely essential to keep the fire burning long after you've said, "I do."

As we wrap up this book, let's briefly look at each part of this biblical definition of love and how it relates to lovemaking.

Love is patient. HI and LO (see chapter 7) both *get* to practice patience in lovemaking. And patience is sometimes required in helping your mate achieve that longed-for "O." Patience really is a virtue in the marital playground.

Love is kind. The goal of sex is to bless your spouse. Does your man like neck kisses? Your woman might melt with a long foot massage. Why not be nice? Indulge your spouse with simple gestures they enjoy.

It does not envy. You can't afford to look at others. Celebrate what is good in your own love relationship, not what another couple has in their relationship that you seem to be lacking in your own.

Isn't it marvelous that God tailor-made you for each other? What you have together is unique and special.

It does not boast. Celebrate your sexual standing stones together in the privacy of your own marriage. You know that your lover is the greatest lover on earth. Your mate needs to know that little tidbit, but your next-door neighbor probably doesn't.

It is not proud. Your skill in lovemaking is a gift from God. Isn't it amazing that our God in heaven even cares about making *you* a great lover?

It does not dishonor others. Complement, encourage, and build-up your mate's ability to share sexual pleasure. Never make fun of your lover's lack of skill in the bedroom. We are all works in progress, so celebrate any improvement in your spouse's lovemaking abilities.

It is not self-seeking. Remember that *agape* love from God centers on the other person's desires and needs. How can you best meet your spouse's needs today? Is your mate's love tank full?

It is not easily angered. Lovemaking supernaturally engenders peace. "Do not let the sun go down while you are still angry" (Ephesians 4:26) is very wise counsel indeed. Make love, not war.

It keeps no record of wrongs. Forgive the failings of the past; embrace your lover fully today. Be known as a person with a crystal-clear memory of things done well.

Love does not delight in evil. Don't be diverted toward darkness. What could be more enjoyable than good, holy sex? Delight yourselves in innocent, fun play. Tag! You're it!

But rejoices with the truth. The truth is that God created you to love and be loved. The truth is that sex as God intended is good, clean fun. Why not share a bubble bath tonight?

It always protects. The playground of marriage is meant to be wholly safe. It is also wild and wonderful, extravagant and sensual—but it is always safe.

Always trusts. The more secure lovers are, the more gratifying sex will be. Remember, it is the people who have been happily married for years that enjoy the best and hottest sex.

Always hopes. Your love life is intended to flourish. How is your love garden growing?

Always perseveres. Lovemaking skills are refined over time. Expect progress and maturing in your own lovemaking skills. Celebrate as you go along. Chocolate-dipped strawberries can be nice even when it is not Valentine's Day.

The Best Way to Make Love

A man once asked Jesus, "Which is the greatest commandment in the Law?" (Matthew 22:36). It was a trick question, of course, considering there were over six hundred laws to choose from. As you've been reading *Lovemaking*, we have a similar question for you: Which of the following is the most important aspect of lovemaking?

- Play
- Liberate
- Communicate
- Entice
- Explore
- Imagine
- Satisfy
- Adapt
- Embrace

The answer to this question is the same Jesus gave. His response is enlightening and applicable to everything we have shared with you throughout this book. Jesus said that all the Law can be summed up as follows: to love God extravagantly and to love others intimately (Matthew 22:37–39). Jesus went even further, however, saying, "Contained within these commandments to love you will find all the meaning of the Law and the Prophets" (Matthew 22:40 TPT).

The surest way to enjoy extravagant intimacy in marriage isn't any we've listed above. The most important thing you can do, in life and in the bedroom, is to *love* God and *love* your spouse. You will find meaning in all we have discussed in this book when you put into practice these two commandments, which can be summed up in a single word, namely, love.

> *There is no substitute for God's authentic, pure, holy, astonishing love. His love is the fuel supplying the fire of sexual passion in marriage.*

It lasts for a lifetime. *Love never fails.* And it is deeply satisfying. This love is unrelenting. As you embrace perfect love from the Lover, you will be transformed to experience the ultimate in lovemaking with your spouse.

DR. DAN'S PRESCRIPTIONS FOR LOVE

Practice expressing emotions in your play sessions:

* Make love, expressing comfort and security.
* Enjoy sex as an expression of adventure and excitement.
* Play together with feelings of bliss.
* Have deeply passionate, ravenously hungry sex.

About the Authors

D r. Dan and Linda Wilson are marriage missionaries. They delight in traveling around the world blessing marriages and sharing about Jesus. Taking the call to support widows and children seriously, they are involved with multiple orphanages and mission projects in several nations. Dan and Linda are cofounders of Supernatural Marriage & Missions, created to encourage Spirit-led intimacy in marriages through conferences, teaching, writing, and personal counseling. They have two sons enjoying their own supernatural marriages and four beautiful grandchildren. The Wilsons reside in Fort Worth, Texas.

Dan and Linda Wilson appreciate receiving any comments you might have about *Lovemaking* or their ministry. They are not able to provide personal counsel via e-mail. However, you can contact them via their website at SupernaturalMarriage.org.

Other books by Dr. Dan and Linda Wilson include *7 Secrets of a Supernatural Marriage* (also in Telugu and Spanish), *CO-: Powerful Partnerships in Marriage*, *Experiencing Supernatural Marriage: A Study Guide*, *Supernatural Marriage: The Joy of Spirit-Led Intimacy* in Spanish and Finnish.

For more information concerning Supernatural Marriage & Missions, to order copies of any of their other books, or for information about attending or hosting a Supernatural Marriage event, please visit...

www.SupernaturalMarriage.org

Acknowledgements

Lovemaking. It has taken more than a little courage as well as much encouragement from many people to get this book up and running.

We first want to acknowledge God as the greatest Lover who inspires us to love as He does—freely and joyfully. We are forever in love with You, Almighty God.

Rissa, Rebekah, Debbie, and Dorota—you were the key intercessors who covered us as we wrote. You women have been strong in spirit and bold in your prayers. We could not have done it without you.

Dr. Wayne Inzer—your medical expertise and godly counsel were invaluable. Mickey's comments were wise and helpful. We celebrate your supernatural marriage.

Dr. Paul Looney—dating back to our medical school days we have loved your artwork and you. The anatomical drawings for this book are a wonderful contribution. A picture really is worth a thousand words. You and Teri are forever in our hearts.

Bob Beaver and Scott Marlar—you guys bless us again and again. Thank you for standing with us through friendship, prayer, and faithfully serving on our board.

Ryan Adair—you have done it again! We really appreciate your editorial skill and your holy appreciation of marriage.

David Sluka—you are amazing! What a delight to have you as our teacher, editor, cheerleader, troubleshooter, and friend. We are grateful.

Carlton Garborg and BroadStreet Publishing—thank you for believing in us. We appreciate you standing up for holiness and joy in marriage. Bless you!

Now to the King eternal, immortal, invisible, the only
God, be honor and glory forever and ever. Amen.
—1 Timothy 1:17

Glossary

Agape: one of the Greek words translated as *love* in the Bible. This is a selfless love that seeks what is best for another person. It is the perfect love of God.

Anorgasmia: the inability to experience orgasm after ample sexual stimulation.

Areola: the circular dark area of skin around the nipple. This tissue is generally larger in a sexually mature woman than in a man. Montgomery's glands and hair follicles cause bumps on the areolar surface.

Bartholin's glands: two small glands left and right of the vaginal opening in women. During sexual arousal, they produce a small amount of oily fluid that moistens the outer skin of the vulva, improving the comfort of initial penile penetration during intercourse.

Cervix: a round structure at the lower end of the uterus. The head of the cervix is about one inch in diameter and protrudes into the deep portion of the vagina. Sperm pass through the cervical canal to meet the egg for fertilization.

Climax: used as a synonym for orgasm, which is the most intense point of sexual pleasure. It is the peak of sexual excitement followed by a decline in arousal.

Cliterate: being knowledgeable in how to navigate the clitoris for the purpose of female sexual arousal and orgasm.

Clitoris: a highly sensitive erectile organ in the female vulva where the labia minora (inner lips) join together, just in front of the ure-thral opening. The clitoris is much larger than might be assumed by observing the portion that is externally visible. Most female orgasms are achieved through either indirect (intercourse) or direct stimulation of the clitoris.

Coitus: insertion of penis into vagina, usually accompanied by rhythmic movements to experience sexual pleasure or to accomplish reproduction. Synonyms for coitus are sexual intercourse, vaginal intercourse, vaginal sex, copulation, and mating.

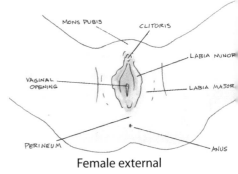

Female external

Copulation: see coitus above.

Cunnilingus: stimulation of a woman's genitals by the lips and tongue for the purpose of sexual arousal. Synonyms for this are oral sex, oral, or oral stimulation.

Digital stimulation: sexual stimulation by use of fingers.

Dopamine: a shortened name for 3,4-dihydroxyphenethylamine, which is a neurotransmitter in the brain that plays an important role in sexual gratification.

Dyspareunia: pain during intercourse. This occurs more frequently in women than in men. There are numerous physical and emotional causes of dyspareunia.

Ejaculation, female: Expulsion of fluid during orgasm secreted by Skene's glands from openings adjacent to the urethra. Female ejaculation is present in a minority of women. The amount of fluid expressed is highly variable.

Ejaculation, male: the release of semen from the penis that is produced by rhythmic contractions of the bulbospongiosus muscle during male orgasm.

Endometrium: a mucous membrane lining the uterus (womb). The endometrium increases in thickness in preparation for embryo implantation, then it is discharged (menstruation) if pregnancy does not occur.

Endorphins: contracted nickname for "endogenous morphine." These are chemicals produced in the brain that create feelings of euphoria similar to those experienced with opium derivatives such as morphine and heroin. Endorphins that are released with orgasm leave men and women with feelings of relaxation and great pleasure.

Epididymis: a coiled cluster of thin tubes attached to the testicle that store sperm. It connects the testicle to the vas deferens.

Epinephrine: a hormone and neurotransmitter, also named adrenaline, that is produced in the adrenal glands and by the ends of sympathetic nerve fibers. Release of epinephrine causes increased heart rate, pulse, blood pressure, and generalized excitement.

Erectile dysfunction (ED): inability to obtain or maintain erection of the penis that is sufficient to allow sexual intercourse.

Erection: the swollen and stiffened state of erectile tissue of the penis, clitoris, or nipples due to sexual arousal. Typically this term refers to the male penis.

Erogenic: see erogenous zone.

Erogenous zone: the areas of the body that are particularly sensitive to sexual stimulation. In general, arousal is accomplished more quickly by stimulating erogenous zones closer to the genitals of both men and women.

Erotic: concerning or arousing sexual desire.

Estrogen: a steroid type of hormone produced primarily by the ovaries in women that stimulates the development of female secondary sexual characteristics.

Fellatio: sexual stimulation by sucking or licking a man's penis. Synonyms for this include oral, oral sex, and oral stimulation.

Frenulum, female: the area where tissue from the two labia minora joins with the body of the clitoris just below the glans clitoris.

Frenulum, male: a band of tissue just below the glans on the front side of an erect penis. This area is a particularly strong erogenous zone in most men.

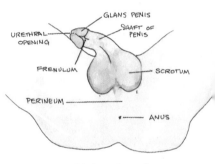

Male external

G-spot: Grafenberg spot. An area in the front wall of the vagina that produces a particularly pleasurable sensation when stimulated. Some scientists believe the G-spot corresponds to the location of Skene's glands adjacent to the urethra. Many women do not seem to have this auxiliary erogenous zone.

Genitals: the externally visible reproductive organs of men and women. A synonym for this is genitalia.

Glans penis: the rounded, spongy tissue at the tip of the penis. If circumcision has not been performed, the glans is partially or completely covered by the foreskin.

Glans clitoris: the highly innervated, spongy tip of the clitoral body. Prior to arousal, a thin flap of tissue, called the clitoral hood, usually covers it.

High plateau: advanced sexual arousal prior to orgasm.

Hymen: thin mucous membrane covering a portion of the vaginal opening.

Hypoactive sexual desire: exceptionally low libido in a man. This sexual disorder is sometimes associated with a low blood level of the hormone testosterone.

Intercourse, anal: inserting a man's penis into an anus for the purpose of sexual pleasure. See chapter 5 for a discussion of the risks involved with this type of intercourse.

Intercourse, vaginal: Entrance of the male penis into the female vagina, which is accompanied by thrusting, often resulting in sexual climax for one or both participants. See coitus above.

Labia majora: also called the outer lips, these prominent skin folds begin at the mons pubis to surround the labia minora. Four inches in length, they come back together at the perineum. The skin in this area contains numerous hair follicles.

Labia minora: the inner lips or folds of skin on either side of the opening to a woman's vagina. Beginning at the clitoris, they extend two to three inches backward to meet with the labia majora at the perineum in front of the anal opening.

Libido: sexual drive, or a desire for sexual activity. Libido is quite variable in both men and women.

Male orgasmic disorder (MOD): inordinate delay or absence of ability to experience orgasm after normally adequate sexual stimulation. Occasional (up to 25 percent of attempts) inability to reach climax is generally considered to be within the range of normal for men.

Masturbation: self-stimulation of the genitals for sexual pleasure, often with the goal of orgasm. This is not necessarily done in private. Masturbation can be performed within spousal view or concurrently with other forms of sexual play (e.g. during intercourse).

Mons pubis: fat pad and skin with pubic hair that covers the pubic symphysis of the pubic bone. The mons is more prominent in women than in men. In women it forms the upper portion of the vulva.

Montgomery's glands: sebaceous glands in the skin of the areola also referred to as areolar glands. They produce oily secretions that protect and lubricate the nipple. These glands enlarge during sexual arousal and become more easily visible.

Oral sex: husband or wife sexually arousing their partner by using lips and tongue to stimulate genitalia. See also fellatio and cunnilingus.

Orgasm: a sudden release of sexual tension resulting in intense muscle contractions in the pelvic region and intense sensations of sexual pleasure. Also referred to as sexual climax, orgasm generally occurs as a result of a period of rhythmic physical stimulation of the penis in men and the clitoris in women.

Internal os: the opening or mouth of the cervix through which the lumen of the uterus connects to the vagina. Sperm enter the uterus after passing through the internal os of the cervix.

Ovary (ovaries): the female reproductive organ (gonad) that produces eggs, estrogen, and progesterone. The two ovaries deposit eggs into the fallopian tubes where they may be fertilized by sperm.

Ovulation: the ripening and discharge of eggs from the ovary into the fallopian tube for possible fertilization.

Oxytocin: a hormone produced in the hypothalamus and secreted by the pituitary gland that stimulates contractions of the uterus during childbirth, release of milk from the breast while nursing, and mother-child bonding. The blood level of this hormone also has been found to rise for both men and women in response to sexual activity. This is thought to promote bonding between spouses in marriage.

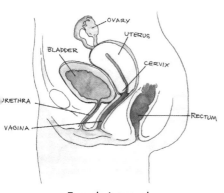

Female internal

Penis: the external male organ of copulation. Internally, the penis contains three columns of tissue that enlarge when filling with blood during sexual arousal (erection). Stiffening of the penis with erection facilitates penetration of the vagina and the discharge of semen (ejaculation) needed for normal reproduction.

Perianal: the skin surrounding the anus is a strong erogenous zone. Stimulation in this area sends sensory signals to the brain via the pudendal nerve, which is the same pathway used for sensations arising from the penis and clitoris.

Perineum: a very sensitive and erogenic area lying between the anus and rear-joining point of the labia majora in women and between the anus and scrotum in men.

Premature ejaculation: coming to male orgasm more quickly than desired. This results in immediate release of semen and soon leads to loss of penile erection, making continued vaginal intercourse difficult or impossible.

Progesterone: a sex hormone produced primarily in the ovaries of women. It prepares the endometrium for implantation of the fertilized egg and maintains a healthy uterine environment for embryonic development. Progesterone also plays an important role in making the female breast ready for milk production after childbirth.

Prostate gland, female: see Skene's glands.

Prostate gland, male: a round gland in men, about the size of a large walnut, that is found surrounding the beginning of the urethra just below the bladder. It secretes a slightly acidic fluid that improves the viability of sperm in the alkaline environment of the vagina.

Refractory period: the time after orgasm in a man during which he cannot be sexually aroused.

Scrotum: the external pouch of skin and muscle in men containing the testes (testicles) that is located below the base of the penis.

Male internal

Semen: the fluid containing sperm cells from the testes, fluid from the seminal vesicles, prostatic fluid, and bulbourethral gland secretion that is released in male ejaculation.

Seminal vesicle: a pair of elongated, saclike glands that secrete fluid that is an important component of semen.

Serotonin: a chemical neurotransmitter that elevates mood and enhances sexual desire. It is common with depression to have a lower-than-normal serotonin level in the brain.

Skene's glands: glandular tissue within the front wall of the vagina that secretes fluid during sexual arousal. This secretion may be released onto the vulva left and right of the urethral opening at orgasm (see ejaculation, female). Similar to the male prostate in microscopic structure, function, and innervation, these glands are referred to by some researchers as the female prostate.

Sperm: male reproductive cell (gamete) produced by the millions in the testicles for the purpose of fertilizing the egg. The sperm cells are combined with various fluids to form the semen that is propelled out of the penis during ejaculation.

Testicle: the male reproductive organ (gonad) that produces sperm cells. The two testes are found within the male scrotum.

Vagina: part of the female reproductive tract; it receives the penis during copulation and expands to expel the baby in childbirth.

Vas deferens: a pair of ducts that carry sperm cells from testicles to urethra during ejaculation.

Vulva: the external female genitals, including the labia majora and minora, the opening of the vagina, and the clitoris.

www.SupernaturalMarriage.org